Computer Aided Architecture & Design

FREDERIC H. JONES PH. D.

William Kaufmann, Inc.
Los Altos, California

10   9   8   7   6   5   4   3   2   1
Printed in the United States of America

Library of Congress Cataloging-in-Publication Data

Jones, Frederic H. (Frederic Hicks), 1944–
   Computer aided architecture and design.

   1. Computer-aided design.   2. Engineering—Data
processing.   3. Architecture—Data processing.
I. Title.
TA345.J63   1986   720′.28′5   86-21337
ISBN 0-86576-102-7 (pbk.)

IBM is a trademark of International Business Machines Corporation

AutoCAD is a trademark of Autodesk, Inc.

CADvance is a trademark of Calcomp.

VersaCAD is a trademark of T&W Systems, Inc.

ei:MicroSpec is a trademark of Eclat Incorporated.

Turbo Designer is a trademark of Creative Technologies Inc.

MicroCAD is a trademark of Imagimedia Technologies Inc.

DataCAD is a trademark of Microtecture Corp.

Design Board Professional is a trademark of Megacad Inc.

AT&T is a trademark of American Telephone and Telegraph Corp.

Omnidraft is a trademark of Omnicad Corporation.

MS-DOS is a trademark of Microsoft Corporation.

dBASE II and III are trademarks of Ashton Tate Corp.

Lotus 1-2-3 is a trademark of Lotus Corp.

Multimate is a trademark of Ashton Tate Corp.

WordStar is a trademark of MicroPro Inc.

Apple is a registered trademark of Apple Computer, Inc.

Xerox is a trademark of Xerox Corporation.

CADapple is a trademark of T&W Systems, Inc.

CADAM is a registered trademark of Cadam, Inc.

CALMA is a trademark of General Electric.

Computervision is a trademark of Computervision, Inc.

ACKNOWLEDGMENTS

This book could not have been realized without the considerable assistance of many individuals and companies. I would like to thank them all. In particular I thank my three "co-authors": Nelson Johnson who wrote most of Chapter 5, Karen Kershaw of Microtecture who provided most of Chapter 3 from the DATACAD manual, and Lloyd Martin who provided most of Chapter 4 from the Turbo Designer manual. Judith Jones helped with the editing, mechanical design and paste-up of the book. The following provided software, examples and assistance: Liz Monroe of Calcomp, Mary Anne Zadfar of Autodesk, Greg La Porte of T & W Systems, Rich Russ of AT&T, Karen Kershaw of Megacadd, Lou Bodnar of Microtecture, William Hooper and Kathy Stark of A.I.A. Service Corporation, Shelley Johnson of Imagimedia Technologies, Robosystems and Digicad. Houston Instruments loaned a DMP-52 Plotter. MAD Intelligent Systems loaned a computer. AT&T loaned graphic cards and equipment. Vermont Microsystems loaned a VMI 8820 graphics card. Howard & Company allowed the use of an Apple Laserwriter. Ted Charter, Jerry Allen, Jack Stiles and many others provided general help. A special thanks is due Mary Borchers of William Kaufmann Inc. for editing and encouragement.

For my friends
Bill Fielder and
Annabelle and David Farmer,
without whose assistance this book
would not have been possible.

CONTENTS

INTRODUCTION   vii

1. CAD AND MICROCOMPUTER CAD   1

What is Computer Aided Architecture 1 □ What is Computer
Aided Drafting and Design 2 □ Historical Overview of the
Field 4 □ The Microcomputer-based CAD System 6

2. CAD CONCEPTS   7

World Coordinate System 8 □ Grid 10 □ Layers
12 □ Symbols 14

3. IMPLEMENTING A CAD SYSTEM   17

How is the Office Organized 17 □ Installation and Training 19
□ A Filing System 23 □ How a Projection CAD is Organized
26 □ How A Drawing on CAD is Organized 29

4. DRAFTING   37

About AutoCAD 39 □ Drawing Walls 42 □ Inserting Doors
60 □ Inserting Windows 62 □ Drafting Symbols 64 □ Inserting
Other Symbols 66 □ Drawing Electrical Plans 68

5. DESIGN   71

Introduction to 3D CAD 71 □ Add-on 3D 73 □ Variety of 3D
Implementations 76 □ 3D System Design Principles 86
□ 3D For the Architect 88

6. SPECIFICATIONS   **99**

How ei:MicroSpec Fits In 101 □ ei:MicroSpec and Specifications 104 □ Flow Diagram 114 □ Design 116 □ Presentation 118 □ Installation Plan 120 □ Elevations 122 □ Symbols 124 □ Master Item List 126 □ Master Category List 128 □ Hardware Specifications 130 □ Hardware Schedule 132 □ Purchase Order 134 □ Master Company List 136 □ Items by Description 138

7. EXAMPLES   **141**

APPENDIX A—HARDWARE   **179**

Computer 180 □ Coprocessors 181 □ Digitizers 182 □ Display Cards 183 □ Mice 184 □ Monitors 185 □ Plotters 186

APPENDIX B—SOFTWARE   **187**

GLOSSARY   **201**

LIST OF PLATES   **219**

Computer Aided Architecture and Design is intended to serve as an introduction to the general concepts of computer aided architecture which includes drafting, specifications and design for architects, designers, facilities managers, engineers and others. It focuses on the leading MS-DOS™ based systems, including AutoCAD™, published by Autodesk, and Cadvance™, published by Calcomp. It also features the specification development program ei:MicroSpec™, published by eclat incorporated. While focusing on these products, it is sufficiently generic to interest anyone considering the purchase of a first microcomputer-based CAD system.

CAD has long been limited to the largest firms. With the sweeping introduction of both low cost hardware and software, the smallest design firm can now afford to enter the field. In fact, it is evident that the long range survivors will be the automated design offices. This book allows the thousands of people who are already sold on the idea of CAD for their profession to evaluate the real life world of microcomputer CAD, before investing $10,000 and hundreds of hours in a system. It serves as a detailed tutorial for the buyer of CAD. The existing ei:MicroSpec, Cadvance and AutoCAD user will also be interested in buying the book to use with the software.

Schools and colleges are rapidly becoming involved with CAD, and are searching for textbooks to support their ventures into teaching CAD within design and architecture programs. This book is appropriate for introductory courses with hands-on hardware, as well as for the programs that have not yet allocated CAD equipment in their budgets.

1. CAD AND MICROCOMPUTER CAD

WHAT IS COMPUTER AIDED ARCHITECTURE?

Computer aided architecture includes CAD drafting, 3D presentation graphics, wordprocessing and database applications such as specification writing and accounting, project managment, etc. The scope of this book is to cover more specifically the development and production of contract documents including drafting, written specifications and project costing and administration.

My intention is to concentrate on affordable microcomputer-based CAD systems, the cutting edge of automated architecture and design. The power of these systems, and their sophistication, rivals that of the mainframe systems of just a few years ago, and they are now within reach of every design office.

WHAT IS COMPUTER AIDED DRAFTING AND DESIGN?

There are many parallels between computer aided drafting and manual drafting. When you begin a design, the computer presents you with a grid similar to the familiar blue gridded drafting paper. You then can use a mouse or digitizer pen to "draw" on the computer screen and, subsequently, save the drawing to a disk memory device. The computer can also provide templates of doors, furniture or other symbols for you to place on the screen, much like a rubber stamp or transfer sheet. There are many standard shapes that can be automatically drawn on the screen such as lines, circles, rectangles, curves, arcs, polygons, ellipses, symbols and text.

The symbols you use to create a drawing may be selected from a standard symbol library, or you may create custom made symbols. They can then automatically be placed anywhere on the drawing and can easily be cloned as many times as you wish. If you change your mind on the design or attributes of a symbol, it can automatically be updated in all the places it has been used; all this requires re-drawing the symbol only once. The standard libraries of symbols can be purchased along with your basic software.

Professional CAD packages allow you to create drawing sets with many layers. The layers may be viewed or plotted individually or in multiples. This is similar to overlay or MiniMax drafting techniques. You can therefore place walls on layer one, furniture on layer two, electrical work on layer three and so on. Using this technique you may design and develop extremely complex drawings in easy-to-understand segments. Confusion is prevented when editing dense sections, and unused sections are not allowed to clutter the workspace. The computer can then concentrate on drawing and updating only the active layers; it is not asked to waste memory and data processing time on unused layers and details. This efficiency is translated into increased drawing speed.

One of the areas of greatest concern for neophytes is the small size of the computer screen versus the larger size of a sheet of drafting paper. The computer screen generally works as if it were a window looking on the world of the drawing sheet. The electronic drafting page could be a mile square, one inch square or any size you define. The computer and the plotter keep track of the scale in which you are drawing and allow you to concentrate on the design itself. The lengths of lines and spacings are displayed on the bottom of the screen, regardless of the scale and screen display size. The operator can zoom in and out of the drawing to edit or view the entire sheet or just a tiny portion of it. The plotter then translates the drawing to any scale and sheet size you choose at plotting time.

The ability to edit, move, copy, rotate, mirror, scale and delete portions or all of a design is probably the most attractive aspect of CAD and can reduce initial drafting and revision time drastically. This particularly holds true on projects with many repeatable parts. The CAD system operates much like a graphic arts version of a word processor. It also allows the designer to store complete drawing files in a small diskette storage box instead of large and heavy drawing files.

Automatic Dimensioning is one of the advanced attributes of CAD. This allows the user to simply point at the beginning and end of a line or object and the computer will automatically provide the dimension line, extensions, arrow heads and the dimensions themselves. The process is simple, fast and extremely accurate.

The Database Extraction option allows the user to assign attributes to symbols including manufacturer, catalog number and price. The software will then count all the places in the drawing that the particular symbol is used and report the quantity. The results are stored in a database for future recall. This has proven invaluable in furniture layouts, construction cost estimating and specification writing. The data can be combined and sorted in many ways to produce reports for cost estimating, specification writing and bid preparation. The system can also generate quick and accurate area calculations.

HISTORICAL OVERVIEW OF THE FIELD

One of the earliest uses of interactive computer graphics was the SAGE Air Defense System in the 1950s which allowed the use of CRT displays to identify targets by pointing at them with light pens. The first serious proposal for interactive graphics was presented by Ivan Sutherland in his Ph.D. dissertation on the Sketchpad drawing system. This included the concept of symbol libraries, pointing and drawing with the light pen and interactive editing. The first serious commercial application was by General Motors which developed multiple time-shared graphic workstations to develop car designs.

The widespread use of CAD was prohibited by great cost of hardware, difficulty of writing complex and large programs within the time-share environment and one-of-a-kind software. These early starts in CAD were followed by mainframe systems represented today by CADAM™, CALMA™, and smaller systems such as COMPUTERVISION™ and AUTOTROL™. Large systems of this type proliferated in large engineering and manufacturing companies, and several of the largest architectural companies began to experiment with the systems. The cost of the hardware, software and other resources still made the widespread use of CAD impossible in the general architectural community.

This all began to change in the late 1970s and early 1980s with the introduction of experimental graphic and CAD systems for the Apple II™ computer, such as CADapple™ by T&W Systems. The real breakthrough came, however, with the introduction of MicroCAD™, written by Nelson Johnson, and AutoCAD, by AutoDesk, for the IBM Personal Computer. At last, usable CAD systems within the reach of the individual architect and designer had arrived. The current industry is growing rapidly, and the capabilities of the new wave of CAD software and requisite hardware are approaching those of the mini and mainframe systems.

Nelson Johnson, AIA, the developer of MicroCAD says:

"A surprisingly short number of years ago engineers were talking about pocket calculators replacing slide rules. The calculators which stimulated so much enthusiasm had *scientific notation* and *trigonometric functions* and we clustered around the desk of the first person in the office to buy one. One cost about $350. In the short amount of time since then, small computers, and now the IBM Personal Computer, have become indispensable.

"In the *old* days we used the calculator to perform one step at a time, and this was an improvement in the sense that calculations were at least devoid of the boring mental exercise of primitive addition, slide-rule precision conversions, etc. With the personal computer we are capable of sharing the design process with the machine. When we make changes in our sequence of calculations we change the portion we want, and all the rest falls into place. MicroCAD functions in this way. You, as designer are free to construct models in three dimensions, or to use the two dimensional aspect of the system for drawing. You have a great deal of control over your models, because you can change the numeric specifications of lines and points in space.

"Transcribing field notes for a survey and visualizing the closing of the traverse, or constructing piping alignments and isometrics, or viewing a building as it would look from an opposing hillside are typical uses to which microcomputer CAD can easily be put. Like the scientific pocket calculator, CAD on the small computer put powerful modeling tools in the hands of the designer. Before such personal tools were available the only recourse for most designers was to use the company mainframe computer, if one was available. Such use involved waiting one's turn, scheduling access time, accounting for expensive computer time and a host of other overwhelming inconveniences, or even more likely doing without."

THE MICROCOMPUTER-BASED CAD SYSTEM

Strengths

The greatest strength of microcomputer-based CAD software is that it allows the single user to inexpensively design, draft and model complex solutions to problems. This can increase creativity and productivity and doesn't require expensive hardware and peripherals. The microcomputer, being a general purpose machine, also can be used by the designer for project management, data manipulation and word processing. Dedicated CAD workstations are not nearly so flexible.

Weaknesses

One of the current weaknesses of the microcomputer-based CAD systems is the slower speed in processing the complex equations and data handling processes required when modeling complex graphics problems. The other major weakness is the relative immaturity of microcomputer CAD software. Large system software has had several decades to develop and unfortunately not all the lessons learned there have been fully applied to the micro world. An example of this is the lack of drawing history and management features present in microcomputer-based products.

2. CAD CONCEPTS

CAD THINKING

One of the biggest objections that designers and architects raise in relationship to CAD is that it is alien to the way they have been used to thinking and drawing, and that it will somehow eliminate the creativity and art from the process of design. While this is possible, I think it is no less likely than that writing will be removed from the author and be replaced by the word processor. The facts as I see and have experienced them are that both word and picture processing eliminate rote and boredom from the process and allow many more options for revision and experimentation than are possible with a pencil or typewriter. The computer is only a tool, no more, no less. People are still in control.

While the designer is still in control of his or her tools, new tools require new strategies. At the turn of the century an architect turned over the basic sketch to the drafters and many meticulous tracings were made of the drawings on linen, and then distributed to the various trades for construction. Even earlier, when a lawyer or business person needed multiple copies of a document, it was turned over to the scribe who copied it ad infinitum. The tracing has been replaced by the technology of the blueprint, and the work of the scribe is done with no complaints by the XEROX™ photocopy machine.

When the designer is drafting with pencil or pen for reproduction by the Diazo machine, a certain graphic style and set of standards are affected in order that the reproductions maintain line quality and read well. This is accommodating the technology. When you are drawing with the computer, you must also take into account line weight and other factors, but with the processing and plotting of the machines in mind. In this section we will cover some of the factors which must be considered.

WORLD COORDINATE SYSTEM

A difficult concept, but one fundamental to the CAD system, is that one is always drawing at full scale no matter what the size the object appears on the screen. In the world of the computer the units and relationships are analogous to the real world. Scale is only apparent when the drawing is plotted onto paper. Theoretically, if your plotter was big enough, you could plot any drawing at full or larger than full size just as well as at a smaller size. When thinking of the drawing, the designer learns to refer to the dimensions provided by the computer and trust that scale will be handled at plot time.

Measurements in the world of CAD are done in relationship to the system of Cartesian coordinates named after French philosopher and mathematician Rene Descartes. The "axes" of the system are X representing length, Y representing width and Z representing height. The numbers which identify the location of a point in space are "coordinates." These conventions allow the designer to orient himself or herself, as well as communicate with others the dimension and spatial relationships of the design.

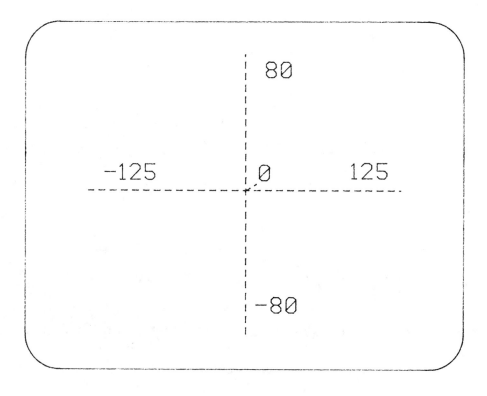

GRID

The grid in a CAD system is analogous to the pre-gridded drafting papers that engineers use. One difference is that in the computer the grid can be set at any size you wish and grids can be exchanged at will during the drawing process to visually guide the task at hand. Another difference is the fact that the grid can be set to "snap," and when you are drawing lines and shapes with a high degree of accuracy, the lines can be made to literally snap to the intersections of the grid lines. This speeds the drawing process and overcomes the tediousness of measuring and scaling. The snap aspect of grids can be present in the drawing process even when the visible grid is turned off. Grids can be made to plot in colors or can be turned off at plot time.

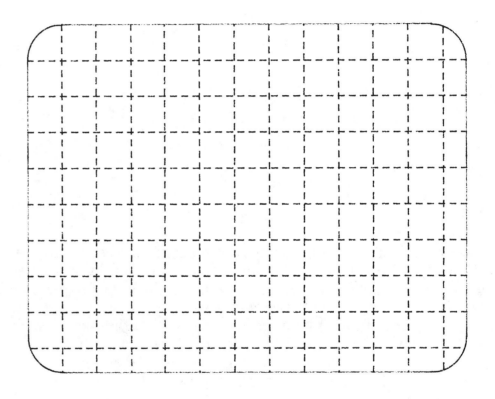

LAYERS

Layers are analogous to the multiple sheets of paper or plastic media that drafters use to contain and segregate categories of information. An example is the convention of making a separate drawing for plan, ceiling plan, electrical plan, etc. Another example which is more direct is the pen register system of drafting, where the base plan is on the master sheet and only the electrical, mechanical and other information is present on subsequent sheets. The final blueprint is made by layering several sheets with coordinated information together and printing them as if they were a monolithic drawing.

The computer can replicate this multilayer concept with a great deal more efficiency, and the computer age drafter and designer can make almost unlimited layers of segregated data with no concern for graphic degeneration. This capability allows the designer to not only organize drawings more easily and efficiently, but also to organize data for sorting, retrieval and analysis.

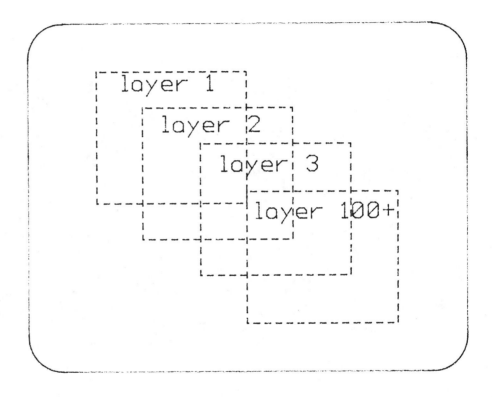

SYMBOLS

"Symbols" are analogous to the plastic furniture, door and plumbing templates you use when drafting manually. Symbols are created as little drawings of any complexity and are stored in the computer's memory to be recalled, inserted and copied into new drawings at will. This process allows objects to be drawn only once and also allows the computer to count the location and frequency of the items for reports such as bills-of-materials.

PLUMBING FIXTURES

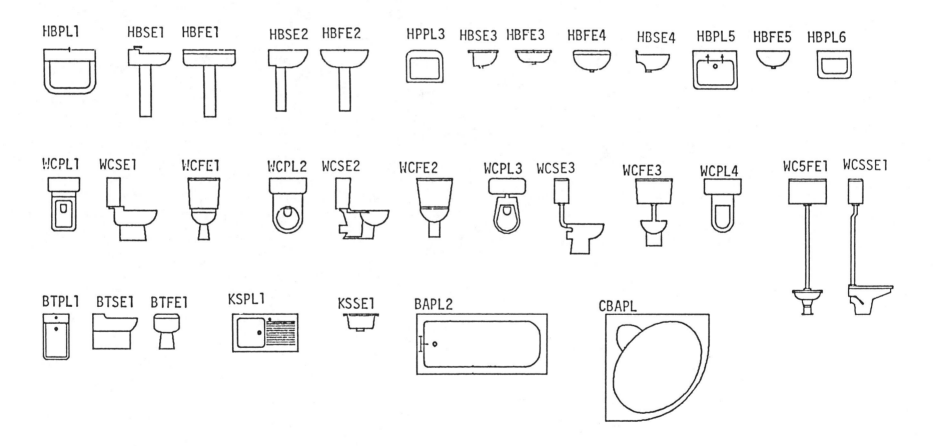

3. IMPLEMENTING A CAD SYSTEM

This chapter is a condensed version of the CAD strategy chapter from the DataCAD™ user's manual published by Microtecture Corporation. It is used with their permission though I will take full responsibility for errors or ommissions. We will cover here both the process of organizing the design office for the intrusion of CAD as well as the basics of organizing your drawings and projects produced on the computer.

HOW IS THE OFFICE ORGANIZED?

Converting an office from manual drafting to computer aided design solves many existing problems at the same time it creates new ones. Gains in drafting productivity and the ability to explore more creative possibilities in a given amount of time can be offset by manager-employee friction caused by the introduction of unfamiliar tools and methods into what was previously a familiar, technologically simple environment. The method of producing drawings has stayed pretty much the same for a couple hundred years--to change that method successfully means being sensitive to the potential impact of change on those involved, and it means making the new method parallel the old method as closely as possible. That's our intention here: to replace the old tools with new ones without disrupting the designer at work.

Assumptions

Production in design offices is based on putting the pencil to the paper and drawing the building, but the way that drawing is compiled into a set of drawings varies greatly from office to office. In making our transition from manual drafting to CAD, we will assume the following strategies already exist in your office:

1.   Systems Drafting. Systems drafting is the process of producing a set of construction documents by first producing individual drawings composed of several overlaid pieces of paper called "layers," then assembling those drawings into drawing sheets by laying them out on a flatbed printer and making a sepia mylar of the layout. The sepia mylars are then given sheet numbers and assembled into the final set.

Though systems drafting may not be familiar to you, it is a process which has strong corollaries to computer aided design. We will explain the computer aided drawing process more completely later in this chapter.

2.   Manager/Drafter Teams. Office productivity is based largely on the degree of cooperation and communication which exists between project managers or job captains and designer/drafters in planning out drawing tasks and then executing drawings. This relationship becomes more critical when using computer aided design simply because one draftsman is now capable of simultaneously producing his or her own drawing and several parts of other drawings which may be under development elsewhere in the office. Proper management of the drawing process will allow drafting redundancy to be kept to a minimum. We will further describe the implications of proper management in the sample problem at the end of this chapter.

INSTALLATION AND TRAINING

First impressions can be lasting impressions. Whether CAD is perceived positively or negatively by your office staff may well depend on your attitude towards the system and toward your employees, and may also depend upon the first experience each employee has with trying to draw on a computer. You will want to maximize excitement and interest and minimize frustration and discouragement.

One approach to discussing CAD installation and training is to mention right off the bat what *not* to do when introducing a CAD system into your office.

Don't install a CAD system two weeks before a huge set of working drawings are due, hoping to finish a week in advance.

Don't begin your first project on a complicated hospital or a re-design of the space shuttle.

Don't expect a 20.1 percent productivity gain in the first project.

Don't lock your employees in a room with nothing but a strange computer and a loudly ticking time clock.

Now here are some things you *should* do:

Do find one or two people who are going to spearhead the transitional effort. Give them plenty of machine time to learn the program and develop their own proficiency before introducing the system to everyone else.

Do consider providing some professional computer training for those first learning the system. The investment of time and money will be quickly recouped in a lower level of frustration and a dramatic improvement in the learning curve. Sometimes all that's needed is a graphic demonstration of what is already understood verbally.

Do plan to develop CAD gradually. Select a small, well-defined project with an open timetable for completion. Or, concentrate your efforts on becoming familiar with producing standard types of drawings which can be used for many projects, such as schedules or typical details. Or, concentrate on building a database template library of useful items.

Do keep accurate records of time spent on the CAD system. Follow the productivity curve carefully. When the learning curve has leveled, determine a billing rate for your system.

Do participate with your employees in the learning process. Even if you know nothing about computer aided design, your expertise in producing construction documents will be useful in guiding your designer/drafters in how best to use the system.

Office productivity and employee attitude toward the computer will be related in some way to how the computer is physically integrated into your office. Is the computer a "hands off" item located down the hall in a locked room (so employees won't "play" with it), or is the computer a "hands on" tool located in the drafting room, familiar to everyone and convenient to use? The latter arrangement will enhance optimum use and employee acceptance of the computer as a normal part of the working environment. One of the advantages of using a microcomputer-based system is the elimination of special environments in which the computer must operate. A microcomputer requires no special environmental conditions aside from being located where it isn't raining. The following typical office layout tries to maximize this advantage.

Let's assume the production department of an architectural office is staffed by two job captains and six designer/drafters. We will equip the office with one computer workstation for every two people, or four workstations total. This number is chosen for the following reasons:

1. A designer/drafter in a fully equipped CAD office should have free access to a workstation when he or she needs it. As much as possible, the computer should fit into the drafter's schedule and not vice versa. After all, no manager would expect two drafters to be productive while trying to share the same drafting board. However:

2. CAD workstations are expensive, and not all of each drafter's time is spent drawing. This is even more the case with the job captain, who spends much of his or her time supervising the drafters, checking their work, or planning their tasks. In addition:

3. Strategic use of CAD involves more planning and less drawing than manual drafting. A drafter who plans his or her drawing process can eliminate drafting repetition by utilizing the automatic drawing features of DataCAD. This means somewhat less time is needed on the machine. And finally:

4. Continuous use of a CAD system can be physically and mentally fatiguing. This is mostly a function of staring at a television screen. Some people will fatigue after eight hours or more; others will become tired much sooner.

For all of these reasons, you can plan that each employee will spend an average of four hours a day on the computer. Drafters will spend more than this, job captains less. Hence, install one workstation for each eight-hour work day, or one workstation for every two people.

Notice that in the office layout illustration, the workstation is located between two desks. This is one arrangement that facilitates convenient use of the computer and utilizes the drafter's drawings. You may find that, depending on space limitations, it is more convenient to locate the workstations in one place in the drafting room.

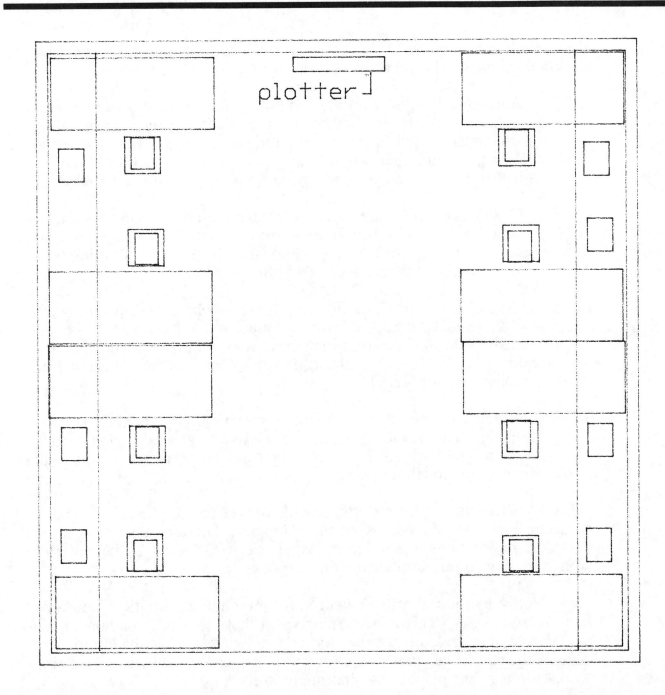

A FILING SYSTEM

How do you keep all these files straight? You will soon find that identifying your drawings, templates, and layers with names like "FLOORPLAN," "BRICKS" or "DIMENSION" becomes confusing and redundant: *Which* floor plan? *What* kind of bricks? Dimensions of *what*?

Despite the fact that everyone would rather read names than numbers, we believe that a systematic numbering system is the best way to name your files in that it eliminates confusion between files and consequently lowers the frustration associated with trying to find a file. How you structure this numbering system is up to you (only you know how systematized your office needs to be). Following is a sample numbering system that has worked in several architectural offices.

How To Name Drawing Files

Drawing files can be named by using seven of the eight characters available in a filename prefix, and dividing those seven characters into three groups corresponding to the following information about the file:

First 3 characters = last 3 digits of office job number

Next 2 characters = letter and number for type of drawing

Last 2 characters = chronological number of drawing

Now here is a suggested system for identifying *types* of architectural drawings. Structural, mechanical, HVAC and civil drawings can be identified by type in a similar fashion:

A0 = general (index, symbols, location plan, 3D views)

A1 = existing and temporary conditions, site work, demolition

A2 = plans, details plans, roof plan

A3 = exterior elevations, detail elevations

A4 = building sections, wall sections

A5 = interior elevations, toilet elevations

A6 = reflected ceiling plan, floor patterns, furnishings

A7 = schedules, door and window types

A8 = details

A9 = alternates

For example, if we were about to start drawing the fourth elevation to be produced in job number 85236, the drawing would be named:

236A304.CAD (or .VWF, .DWG, etc.)

File Management

Let's review for a moment our typical office setup. We have provided four independent workstations and a central storage location for floppy disks. We've determined how to keep track of all the files that will be created on the workstations, and we've learned how to copy those files from the workstation hard disk onto floppy disks so that we can transfer files from workstation to workstation, and make backup copies of files to keep stored in a centrally located "card catalog" of floppy disks.

Assuming you have an office setup similar to the one outlined here, and assuming you have devised a system to keep track of your files, such as we have done, then efficient file management can be accomplished by following three simple rules:

1. Each drawing file contains only one drawing, unless the project is very small. This allows many people to work on different parts of the same project, and keeps "refresh time" to a minimum.

2. All drawing files are stored on floppy disks, so each workstation hard disk contains only layer and template files (your library of often-used items).

3. To work on a drawing, a drafter takes a floppy disk from the box and copies a drawing file onto his or her workstation, where the necessary changes to the drawing are made. When the changes are completed, the drawing file is copied back to the floppy disk and the floppy disk is returned to the box.

This process is analogous to the familiar office practice of working on different drawings throughout the day by removing them from drawers and taping them down to the drawing board. It also means that there is *always* a backup copy of the drawing file (on the hard disk of the workstation where the file was last used), but there is *only one authorized version* of the drawing file (on the floppy disk). So if Bob works on the drawing at his own desk today, but is sick tomorrow, Ann can take the drawing file with Bob's changes to her own desk and keep working on it. When Bob returns, Ann's changes are recorded on the disk which Bob takes to his desk to continue working.

From time to time you make backup copies of the entire contents of the box of floppy disks. To do this you may want to purchase an external hard disk drive (which can store from 20 to 40 million bytes) and make backups onto large-memory tape cartridges to store in a bank vault or other safe location. Otherwise you can simply make a copy of every floppy disk, and store the backup floppies in a safe place. Backups should be done once a day, once a week, or once a month, depending on the volume of work you are producing on your CAD system.

HOW A PROJECT ON CAD IS ORGANIZED

As a project manager you are given a design and production task of a certain scope, which must be completed within a given time frame using the resources at your disposal, those resources being talented people who are properly using well-designed tools.

How well is your office organized to produce projects? Before we discuss how to produce a project on CAD, you may want to review your own office production process. Below is a quick checklist for your consideration. If there are some unanswered questions here, it may be time for some organizational effort. If you have been using overlay drafting techniques in your office, this task will become easier.

Do you have well-defined responsibilities for each person on the project?

Is the project manager responsible for drawing organization and sheet layout, or do you let anyone do this?

Who schedules the timing and content of each drawing sheet?

Do you keep an updated list of who is working on each drawing and the stage of completion for each drawing sheet?

Do you provide "sepias" of the building layout to your consultants? Are these made before the inevitable floor plan changes?

Who is responsible for coordinating the working drawings with the project specifications?

Are you using standardized details?

Who is responsible for maintaining the detail library?

Are your drawings indexed to details adequately?

Scope: Plan Your Drawing Layout

A good exercise whether or not you are using a CAD system is to spend some time thinking about the finished set of construction documents. This should be done by the project manager before people begin drawing lines and writing specifications.

Layout each sheet and determine the content and organization of each drawing.

Determine major buliding section and elevation layouts.

Assign sheet numbers for you and your consultants.

Standardize the format for detail and drawing sheets.

Resources: Schedule Personnel and Equipment

Once you have determined the scope of your project, determine who will be working on the project and whether or not they will be using the computer for part or all of their work. Here are some points to consider:

Who is best qualified to work on this particular project? Have these people been trained on the computer?

How well has the computer been integrated into your office? Have you already produced similar, but smaller, projects on the system? In light of this, would producing this project on CAD be a cinch, a challenge, or a catastrophe?

Are there certain parts of this project which, for the time being, would be better drawn manually, given employee experience and expected time of completion?

How many computer workstations do you have? How many people

are needed for this project? Do you have enough equipment to produce the project on the computer?

How well developed is your database of previously drawn items? Are there large parts of this project which are similar to previously drawn projects? Can you make use of your template files to produce details and schedules?

Remember, a principal advantage of CAD is to make efficient use of *everything* that has been previously drawn on the system. Your organizational expertise will determine the proficiency of the system.

Process: Plan The Project Development

As we have mentioned before, two points are key in producing a CAD project smoothly and efficiently:

1. Managers and drafters must communicate with each other.

2. Drafters can produce more than one drawing at a time and should be encouraged to do so.

When drawing with a CAD system, parts of one drawing become the "seeds" of other drawings. For example, the perimeter of the first floor plan is also the roof plan and the outline of the reflected ceiling plan. But this doesn't work so well if the person drawing the perimeter of the first floor plan has cut openings in the walls before copying those walls to the roof plan drawing--no one wants a roof plan with windows in it.

This is a good illustration of the two points mentioned above. The manager needs to tell the drafter which other drawings he or she should keep in mind and what is needed for those drawings, as the drafter is encouraged to make other uses for his or her drawings as the project progresses--uses which the project manager may not have thought of but which could save considerable drawing time.

HOW A DRAWING ON CAD IS ORGANIZED

Up to this point we have been considering what is necessary to produce the CAD project as a whole. Our advice has been directed toward project managers and partners (although we hope designers and drafters have been listening). Let's now narrow our scope of discussion to consider how to produce an individual drawing on a single computer workstation. In doing so we will re-direct our attention to the drafter or designer who must actually draw the building (although we hope the project managers will be listening).

Know All You Can Before You Draw

CAD is very flexible in terms of allowing you to change what you have drawn, and undoubtedly much of your work on the system will be involved with altering drawings which are under design development. Nevertheless, the more information you get right the first time you draw something, the less time you will spend making revisions.

Unlike manual design development, which produces drawings by first sketching the rough idea of the object in mind, then gradually refining this idea into a drawing which is dimensionally and materially specific, CAD produces a drawing which is accurate the first time it is drawn. The drawing is accurate either to the right dimensions or to the wrong dimensions, depending on whether or not the drafter knows the size of the building when he or she draws it.

This suggests that the ideal process of CAD development is just the opposite of manual design development. Instead of starting from the idea of the building and moving down to the bricks, it might be better to start from the brick and build them up into a building. In other words, if you first decide to construct the exterior walls of the building with 8" CMU, then any arrangement of those walls into a floor plan will have accurately drawn walls (important for automatic dimensioning). But, if you finalize your floor plan before you decide on the exterior wall construction, then in order to use automatic dimensioning, or in order to use your floor plan as a "seed" for wall sections and details, you would have to first change the thickness of all the walls you had drawn (in order to match the correct dimensions). This wall thickness change would in turn impact the interior dimensions of rooms and possibly affect the modular grids of ceiling and floor tile, lighting, etc.

Practically speaking, it would be impossible to predict the exact dimensions and materials of everything in the building before the design is finalized. A realistic goal, however, is to gather as much information as possible about the construction of the building before the design development or construction documents phases of the project begin. This will keep time-consuming changes to a minimum, and still allow the building to be drawn and dimensioned accurately.

Specifically, try to gather as much of the following information as possible before you start drawing:

Scope Of Work. How much needs to be drawn? In what detail? What information can be drawn once for several drawings?

Dimensions. What are the basic dimensions of the structural grid, columns, and load-bearing partitions? What size are the interior partitions? Doors and windows? Sill and jamb conditions? Floor and ceiling heights? Joist sizes?

Materials. What are the walls made of? What floor system are we using? Roof system? What is the foundation made of?

Previously Drawn Elements. Which typical details can be used for this project? Which templates are available to help you draw? Which drawings from the schematic design phase can be modified and reused? Which parts of your drawing can be used to create other drawings for this project?

Determine What The Drawing File Will Contain

We have suggested previously a system for organizing drawings in which a single drawing file contains only one drawing. You may wish to deviate from this rule, especially when doing small projects or projects which will be drawn almost entirely by one person.

If a drawing file contains more than one drawing, try to group similar drawings together. One file might contain plans, another elevations, a third details, and so on. Be careful that you do not make your files too large. Large files take more time to load and save, and limit drawing flexibility.

In any case, try not to fill a file with more information than you can copy onto a floppy disk (either 360K or 1.2MB). If your file size exceeds the capacity of a floppy disk, you will need to make backup copies of the file using the "backup" and "restore" commands in DOS instead of the "copy" command in DOS. In practice, "backup" and "restore" have been known to be less reliable than "copy." There is thus the chance with an extremely large file that you will not be able to recover the information from your floppy disks. This does not make clients happy.

Plan Your Drawing Layers

In computer aided design, "layers" are the electronic equivalent of overlaid pieces of tracing paper each containing a small part of the drawing information. The key to good CAD efficiency is well-planned use of the almost unlimited number of drawing layers available to isolate related lines, details and text. There are several factors to consider in deciding how layers are to be organized:

Seed Layers. This term is used to describe any layer that may be used to create the basis for subsequent layers. An example of this is the basic perimeter plan of a multi-story building. This plan might contain (on four layers, respectively) the perimeter walls and bearing walls, the columns, the column center lines, and the common core elements. These layers would be the seeds for the partitioning layout on the third floor, which in turn could become a reflected ceiling plan or HVAC layout for the third floor. Seed layers should be kept as generic and uncluttered as possible.

Refresh Time. The computer's speed determines the amount of time it takes to redraw all the lines displayed on the screen. Since you will be changing scales and views frequently, you will want to minimize the "system overhead" associated with this refresh. Only layers that are turned 'ON' are processed for the refresh. If the layers are organized in such a way as to display only the essential information required for the drawing task, system overhead will be minimized. If you are working on a reflected ceiling plan, for example, there is no need to have site information displayed on the screen. Refresh time will also be affected by how much information you put on each layer. A drawing containing many layers of a few lines each will refresh faster than one containing a few layers with many lines each. Thus it is better to have too many layers than too few.

Before you begin drawing, it is a good idea to sit down and make a list of all the layers you intend to create, noting what you expect each layer will contain. Although creating layers is easy, you will find it helpful to have a reference list as you draw to help you chart your drawing process. This way, when you get interrupted by six phone calls, you'll have an answer to the question, "What was I going to do next?"

This list will also be helpful in ordering your priorities as to what should be drawn first, second, third, etc., in order to make the most of your drawing information.

Know Where To Get Your Drawing Information

Just as your drawing can contribute to the drawing of others, what has already been drawn by others can help you. As you plan your drawing layers, make a note of where you can get some of the basic information needed for your particular task. There's no need to redraw all those toilets for the third floor if they've already been drawn for the first floor, or if you already have an appropriate toilet symbol.

Prioritize Drawing Tasks

As well as making a list of all your layers, you may want to make a flowchart of your drawing process--what to draw first, second, third, etc. While this might be a waste of time with manual drafting, it is not with CAD.

In order to keep drawing redundancy to a minimum, you will want to draw those parts of your drawing that are the most general first, then proceed to gradually detail your drawing until what was general becomes specific. Along the way you will make copies of certain parts of your drawing that can be used for other drawings. But as we mentioned above, you can't spin off the roof plan from the exterior wall drawing if you've already put windows in the exterior wall.

Notice that the process of drawing from the most general to the most specific is the opposite to the process of gathering information to prepare for drawing. You want to understand the building in the greatest detail possible before you draw it. But once you start drawing, you want to document all that information gradually, arriving at the most specific drawing (the detail) only after you have graphically described all the general conditions.

Draw As Few Lines As Possible

A drawing will of necessity contain many lines. The idea behind CAD is to have the computer automatically draw as many of those lines as possible. CAD usually incorporates several functions which make this automation possible. Without going into detail, let's identify the primary functions which multiply your efforts:

Copy. Any line, shape, or area you draw can be copied one or several times automatically. Don't draw the same column fifty times! Draw it once and tell CAD to copy it forty nine times for you.

Mirror. Any line, shape, or area you draw can be flipped and copied at once to produce a mirror image next to the original image. So you only need to draw one side of a corridor of rooms, for example.

Templates. Any line, shape, or area you draw can be stored as a "symbol," or "template". You can draw a tree once, put it in a template, then dot trees all over your site plan just by touching all the places in you drawing where you want the trees to appear.

Know All The Tricks To Change What You've Drawn

Even the best laid plans of mice, men, and architects are subject to client review, and that means change. CAD provides you with many ways to modify anything you have drawn without having to redraw it. Here are some of these functions and tricks:

Stretch. Stretch allows you to surround any area or identify any point and move whatever you've selected to a new location, automatically stretching or shrinking everything attached to what you've decided to move. For example, you can move a window to a new place in the wall, and the wall will be automatically corrected to match the new position of the window.

Change. Change allows you to alter the characteristics or "attributes" of any line, shape or area you've drawn. For example, you can change a wall from double weight solid lines to single weight dashed lines, alter its height from 8 feet to 10 feet, change its color from green to blue, etc.

Move. Move is different from Stretch in that *only* the lines, shapes, or areas you select are moved to a new location in the drawing; everything *connected* to those items stays where it is. So if you have two cased openings, one of which contains a door, you can move the door to the other cased opening if necessary without moving all the wall and jamb lines attached to the door.

Keyboard Shortcuts. As you become familiar with CAD, you will find that you draw with one hand on the mouse (to make lines) and the other hand on the keyboard (to change menus). Keyboard shortcuts for going from one menu to another will allow you to change your drawing options *without interrupting a line you are drawing*. For example, you can start a line and change the snap grid, the line type, the line color, your display scale, and the layer on which you are drawing the line, without ever moving your hand from the mouse and without accidentally ending the line you are drawing.

4. DRAFTING

The most universally accepted use of the graphics aspect of computer aided architecture and design is computer aided drafting. This chapter will give you the flavor of establishing and developing a set of plans and details with one of the most popular CAD software packages, AutoCAD. It also shows how the configuration system Turbo Designer™ is used with the basic AutoCAD system.

My intention is not to teach AutoCAD or to restrict the reader to techniques unique to that system, but rather to allow a look over the shoulder of the CAD system operator as he or she uses a typical system in a real world situation. The Turbo Designer/AutoCAD system is also linked to the ei:MicroSpec specification management and development system to ultimately create the total set of contract documents. Many of the techniques and all of the concepts covered here are quite applicable to any other microcomputer drafting system.

The drawing development process is a complex one, as is the process of using as sophisticated a software system as CAD. No one should be misled into thinking that it is a process requiring little commitment to learn. On the other hand, a few weeks of serious use in the office will produce amazing results. The learning curve on most systems ranges from 40 to 80 hours of use to produce the magic one-to-one productivity ratio with manual drafting. During revisions this leveraged even further in repetitive tasks and when linked with specifications. During revisions the productivity gains jump by an order of magnitude. It is well worth the investment from a productivity perspective.

When using this chapter, please put it into context by referring to Chapter 6, Examples, to see actual projects and drawings which have been developed on various CAD systems. The final test is trying your own hand at CAD. Find a friend or dealer who will let you play with a system for a few hours, and you will be amazed.

ABOUT AutoCAD

AutoCAD is an extremely powerful CAD system--it has features that rival those found on dedicated minicomputer CAD systems that cost over $100,000. Almost anything that can be conceptualized and drawn by hand in two dimensions can be drawn with AutoCAD significantly faster and with a much greater degree of accuracy. AutoCAD's real power, though, comes with the drawing of repetitive elements and in drawing revisions. For instance, drawing a building elevation with a large number of identical window elements can be very tedious and time consuming. With AutoCAD, however, it can even be fun. Simply draw one window to the degree of detail required, define that window as a *BLOCK, INSERT* that block at the appropriate spot in the drawing and then create an *ARRAY* of that window detail of whatever quantity and spacing that that window element requires. What may have taken a draftsman hours to produce by hand can now be done with AutoCAD in a matter of minutes. Although AutoCAD is a very powerful CAD system, it has one major drawback--it is a general purpose CAD system. Because AutoCAD is a general purpose system it is equally suitable for a machine designer as for an architectural designer--it understands the language of drafting, but it does not know the special syntax or procedures for any specialized types of drafting. Because of this drawback (it is not a flaw), a lot of initial preparation by the individual user must be done with AutoCAD before it can be used to anywhere near its full potential.

Turbo Designer is a drawing environment for AutoCAD that enables anyone who produces architectural drawings to draw them faster and with less preparation than can be done by using AutoCAD alone.

Here are some of the features of Turbo Designer: Everything that is scale dependent such as text, dimensioning, linetypes and drafting symbols have been preconfigured to all of the standard architectural scales (no guessing on how the finished drawing will look); It contains a library of over 300 different architectural symbols and details; Also included is a layer management system that assists in keeping track of what is drawn on which layer.

Turbo Designer adds many additional commands to AutoCAD that increase its efficiency for architectural users. For example, walls can now be drawn at any thickness and at any angle in one step (two parallel lines). Doors and windows of any type and size can be inserted into walls of any thickness and at any angle (for the doors, an opening is automatically made in the wall as the door is inserted). Turbo Designer also has the ability to define and insert storefront and curtainwall window systems. A function that allows the user to edit drawing text with a word processor and to later insert it into the drawing using any available style of text is also included.

The heart of the Turbo Desiger system is the Turbo Designer Tablet Menu. This six color tablet menu is divided into two parts. The first part contains virtually all of the AutoCAD commands that are used on a general basis. Each of the different command types is assigned its own color code. Numerous AutoCAD commands have been enhanced and clarified for faster drawing speed. For instance, to zoom in on a window simply pick *ZOOM window* instead of going through three screen menu commands to do the same thing.

The other part of the tablet menu contains all of the specialized commands and details that relate to architectural drafting (some of which were mentioned above).

The tablet menu is used with a digitizer tablet. A digitizer tablet is used for accurately entering graphic data into a computer and it consists of a "drawing surface" (usually 12"x12") and a stylus (pen) or a cursor (looks similar to a "mouse"). A digitizer tablet works similarly to a mouse, in that what you "draw" on the tablet with the cursor will show up on your computer screen. The main difference between a mouse and a digitizer is that a mouse position is always relative, whereas with a digitizer tablet the coordinates on that tablet are always the same to within 1/1000 of an inch.

In order to give you the flavor of how Turbo Designer is used with AutoCAD in architectural drafting, we will go through the process of producing a simple residential floor plan.

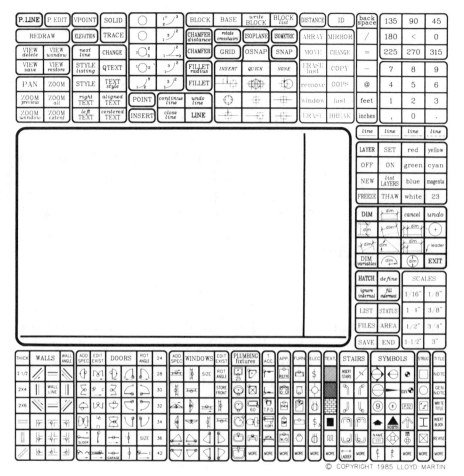

TURBO DESIGNER'S SIX COLOR TABLET MENU

© COPYRIGHT 1985 LLOYD MARTIN

Refer to the Turbo Designer Tablet Menu shown above to follow the CAD example.

DRAWING WALLS

The eight boxes surrounding the box labeled WALL LINE are the various wall line combinations that can be drawn (plus three in the lower left hand corner of the wall section). Each box has a thick line and a thin line. The thick line is the line that you actually draw and the thin line is the line that is the other side of the wall. Normally (but not always) the thick line represents the outside of the wall and the thin line is the inside of the wall.

Drawing walls is very simple. First, pick the box labeled 2x4 with the digitizer stylus or cursor; this sets the current wall thickness for 2x4 stud walls and assumes that the total finished wall thickness is 4-1/2 inches. Next, pick the north wall line BOX (above the box labeled WALL LINE) and set the crosshairs towards the upper left hand corner of your drawing sheet on the screen.

Press the pick button on the cursor or stylus for the beginning of the wall line. Draw a line to the right 46 feet long using the coordinates on the upper right hand corner of the screen as a guide and press the pick button. Now, pick the east wall line BOX on the tablet menu and then, picking the WALL LINE BOX (this will start your next wall at the end of the previously drawn wall), draw a wall down the screen 26 feet long and press the pick button to terminate the line.

Repeat this procedure for the other two walls, and in less than a minute, you have drawn your exterior walls as shown in **Figure 1.**

Figure 1

The next thing to do is to draw layout lines on another layer to assist in drawing the interior walls as shown in **Figure 2.**

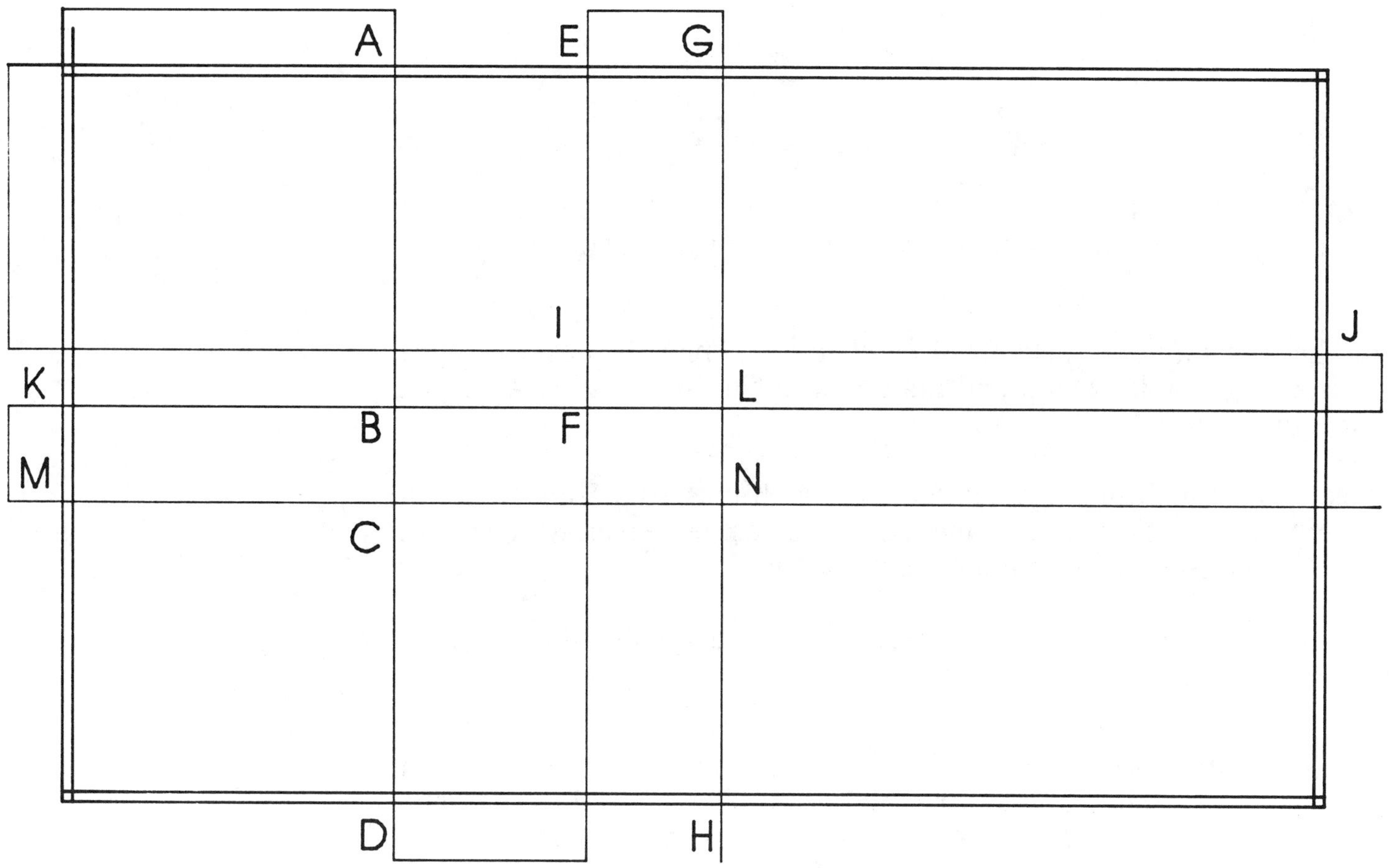

Figure 2

We can draw the main interior walls by using the layout lines as a guide.

Set the Current Layer back to FLOORPLN and pick the east (or right) wall line from the Tablet Menu and draw a wall line from point A to just past point B on **Figure 2**.

Pick the east wall line again and draw a wall line from point C to just beyond point D. Don't worry if the wall intersections overlap--the wall corners will be adjusted later with other commands.

Continue to pick the east wall line BOX and draw walls from points E to F, from points G to L and from points N to H.

Now, pick the north wall line from the Wall Menu and draw a wall from I to J. Continue to pick the north wall line and draw a wall from points K to L, and from points M to N slightly overlapping all of the wall intersections. Finally turn OFF the LAYOUT Layer by picking the green LAYER box, picking the box below it labeled OFF, picking LAYOUT from the Screen Menu and finally pressing <return> on your cursor to end the LAYER command. Your drawing should now look like **Figure 3.**

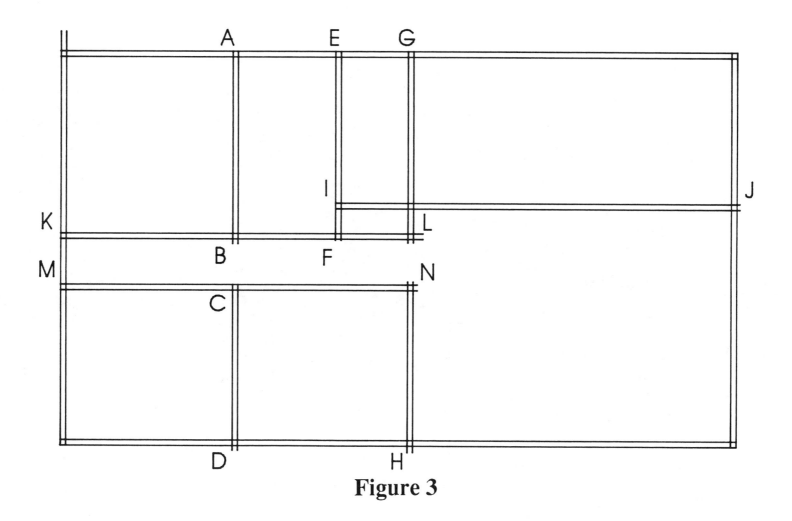

Figure 3

Setting Up View Windows

The next thing to do is to draw the rest of the interior walls. At this point it would be best to zoom in on smaller portions of the floor plan to make it easier to draw in more detail. The easiest way to do this is to divide the floorplan into views as shown in **Figure 4**. This is done by picking the *VIEW window* command, assigning a name to a view and finally picking the two opposite corners of a box that would inscribe the view that you have chosen.

Now, everytime that you want to work on a smaller section of the drawing that was defined as a view, all you have to do is call up that view with the *VIEW restore* command.

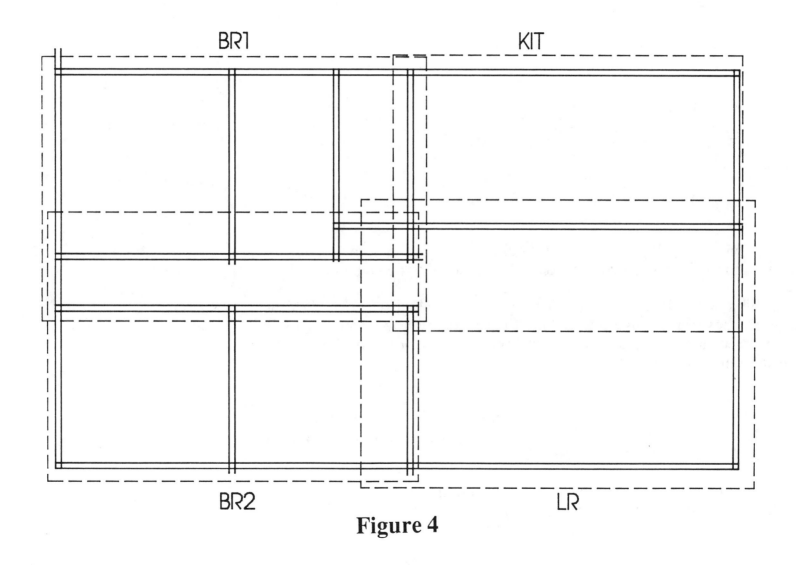

Figure 4

Now we will *ZOOM* in on a smaller portion of the drawing, by picking the *VIEW restore* command and draw some of the smaller walls.

First we will draw a line from the west wall just above the lower closet as shown in **Figure 5** (the dotted line) exactly 8 feet long. This line will be used as a guideline to locate the exact starting point for drawing wall P (8'0" center to center).

Next, we will pick the east wall line box and then pick the WALL LINE box from the Tablet Menu. The start of wall P will now be at the end of the layout line that has just been drawn. Wall P continues south until it overlaps the wall as shown in **Figure 5**.

Finally, using the appropriate wall line commands, walls O,Q,R and S are drawn as shown in **Figure 5** using layout lines and the coordinates in the upper right hand corner of the screen as a guide.

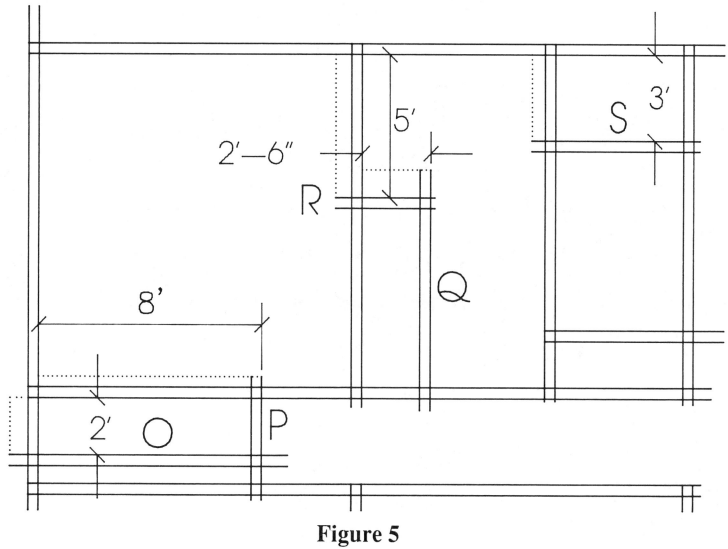

Figure 5

Trimming Wall Intersections

This is a good time to clean up the overlapping wall intersections. At the bottom of the wall section of the tablet menu are nine boxes, each with a drawing of a different type of wall intersection. These commands are used to trim the wall intersections so that the wall lines meet properly at every corner. See **Figure 6**.

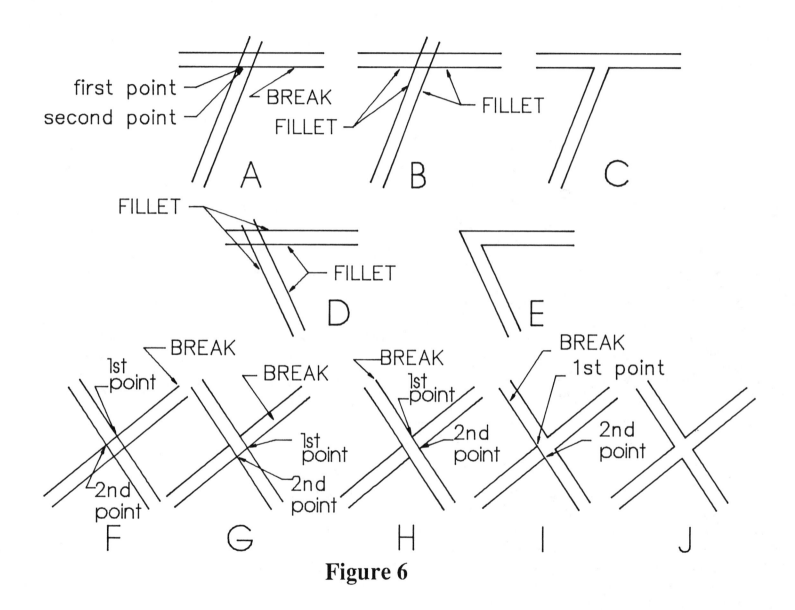

first point
second point

BREAK
FILLET

A

FILLET

B

C

FILLET

FILLET

D

E

BREAK

1st point

2nd point

F

BREAK

1st point

2nd point

G

BREAK

1st point

2nd point

H

BREAK

1st point

2nd point

I

J

Figure 6

Now we will trim the wall corners. First, the wall thickness for the walls that will be trimmed is picked. Next, pick the appropriate corner trimming command for the corner to be trimmed and an aperture (a small square) will appear at the center of the crosshairs. This "square" is set over the intersection that is indicated by the red circle in the command box and when the pick button on the cursor is pressed, the corner will automatically be trimmed. This procedure is repeated at every wall intersection and the drawing will look like **Figure 7.**

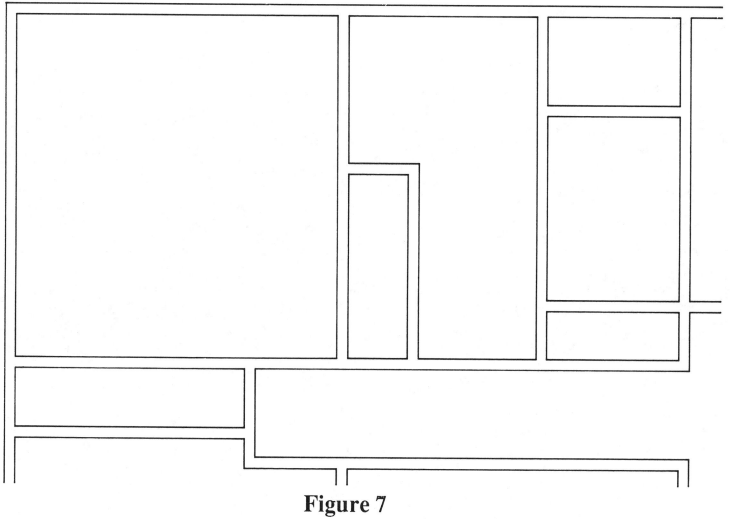

Figure 7

These procedures of drawing walls and trimming intersections are repeated for the remaining three views using **Figure 8** as a guide.

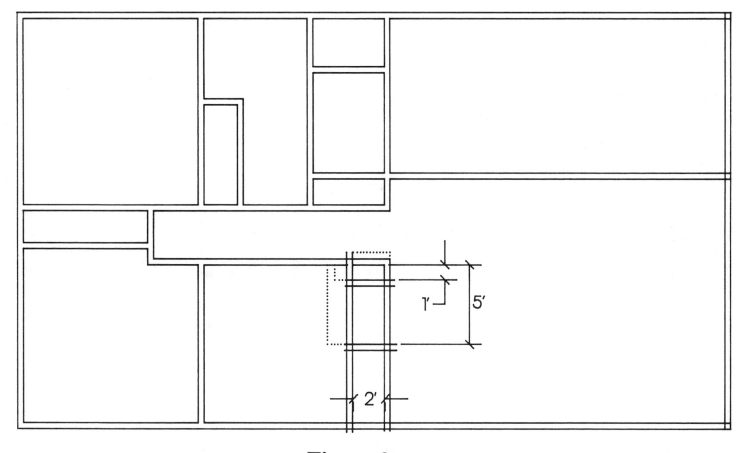

Figure 8

When all of the walls have been drawn and all of the corners have been trimmed in all four views, the *ZOOM extent* command is picked and the drawing will look like **Figure 9**.

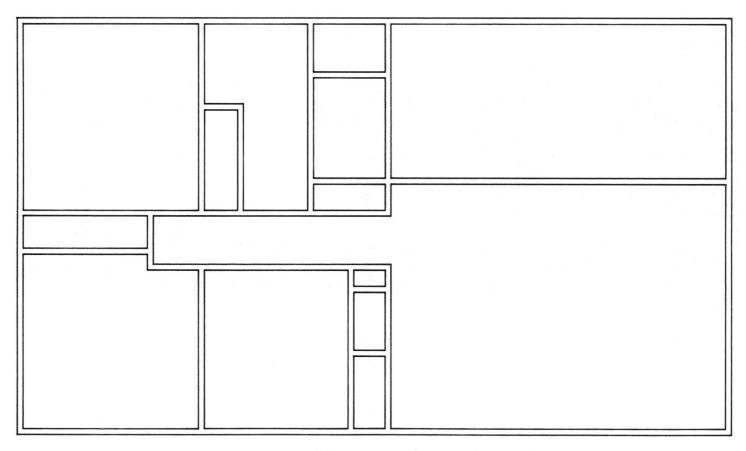

Figure 9

INSERTING DOORS

The second section of the lower Tablet Menu is for inserting doors into walls. Almost any type and size of door can be inserted into any thickness of wall and at any angle.

The type and size of door is first picked; the proper point is chosen for inserting the door into the wall; an opening is automatically made in the wall the exact size of the door; and the chosen door is then inserted into the wall opening. You are then prompted for information regarding that door such as size, door number, item number, etc. (this information is extracted and linked to the bill of materials program that is included with Turbo Designer or with ei:MicroSpec. Let's see, in a little more detail, how doors are inserted into walls.

The first thing to do is to pick *VIEW restore* and return to the BR1 view. Then, the 2x4 wall thickness is picked from the WALL MENU. Next, 32 (for a 2'8" wide door) is picked from the DOOR MENU. Then the correct door is picked from the door menu.

Now the crosshairs are moved to the chosen insertion point on the screen (see the hinge point on Door #1 in **Figure 10**) and the pick button is pressed. Now an opening is made in the wall and the door symbol is inserted into it's proper position.

After specific information about the door is entered, the door number and door size will now be written next to the door that has been inserted into the wall.

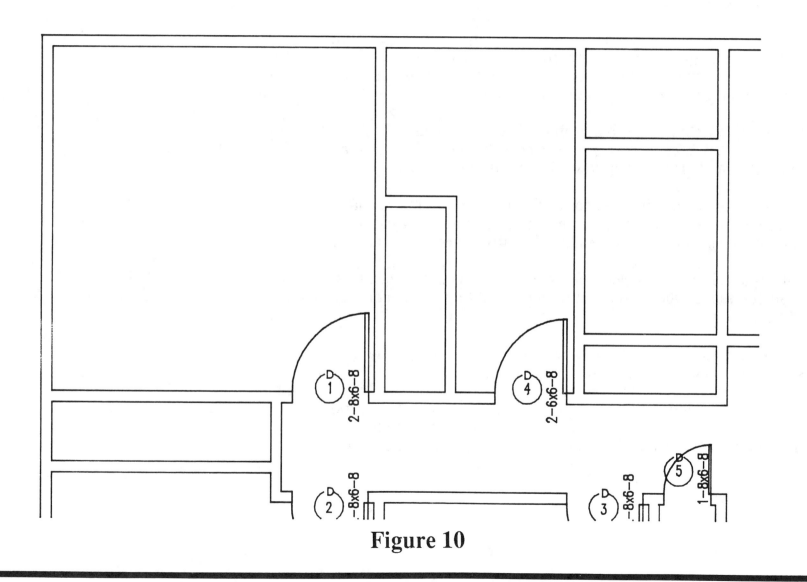

Figure 10

INSERTING WINDOWS

The next section of the Turbo Designer menu contains the window insertion commands.   There are four basic window types that can be inserted. Each window type has one window which is rotatable and it is indicated by the red arrow beneath the window symbol.

There are three other boxes in the Window Menu. The first of these is the box labeled *SIZE*. This box is picked before the appropriate window symbol box, and the total window width in inches is entered.

The next box is labeled *ROT ANGLE*.   This command is for specifying the window angle for inserting a rotatable window into a wall other than the standard orthogonal wall (walls running at 0 and 90 degrees).

Finally, there is a box labeled *STORE FRONT*. This command transfers you to a screen menu where you will be prompted to insert a storefront window system into a wall.

Windows are inserted into walls exactly the same way that doors are inserted into walls. First pick the *SIZE* box and enter the total window width in inches, then pick the desired window box and finally, picking one of the *OSNAP* modes (either *NEAREST* or *MIDPOINT*) pick the insertion point in the wall for the window. The window is then inserted into the wall and you will be prompted for the window specs.   See **Figures 11, 12, and 13.**

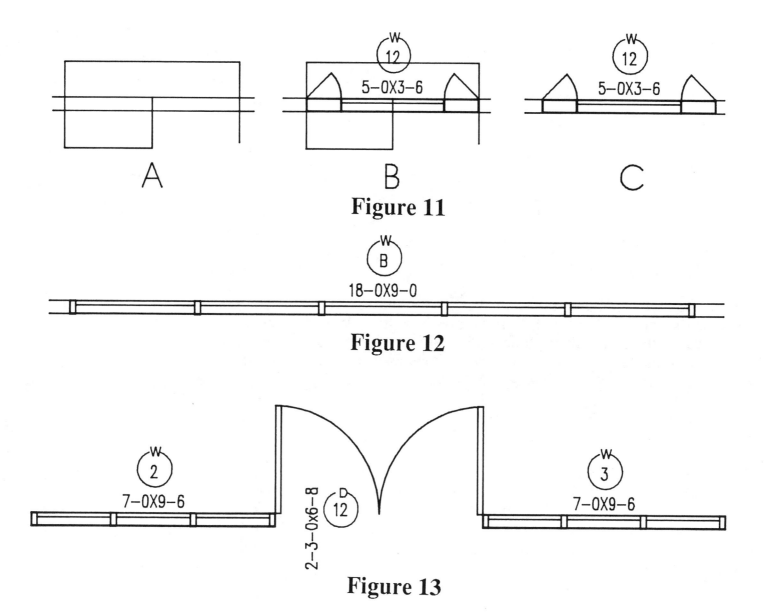

A   B   C

Figure 11

Figure 12

Figure 13

DRAFTING SYMBOLS

Turbo Designer contains many of the most commonly used drafting symbols such as Section Arrows, Detail Title Blocks and Detail Reference Arrows. These symbols are all scale dependent--no matter at what scale the drawing is plotted, these symbols will always be the same size on the finished plot.

As an example of how this works, we will show how a Section Reference Arrow, as shown in **Figure 14**, would be inserted into a drawing.

First the Section Reference Arrow is picked from the Tablet Menu, then the location for the Arrow in the drawing is picked and the desired direction for the Arrow is entered. Next, you are requested for the Section Reference Number and the Section Reference Sheet Number (these numbers are automatically placed in their proper place within the arrow). Finally, the actual Section Reference Arrow (with the reference numbers) is placed in the drawing at the point that you selected.

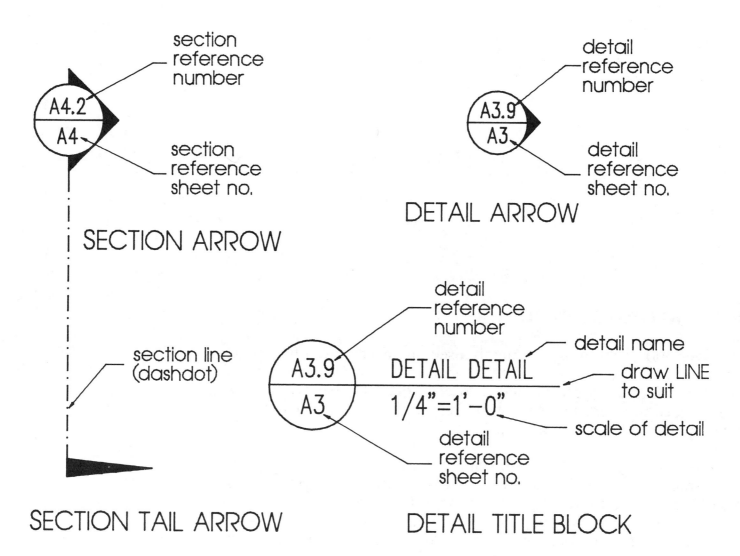

section
reference
number

section
reference
sheet no.

SECTION ARROW

detail
reference
number

detail
reference
sheet no.

DETAIL ARROW

section line
(dashdot)

SECTION TAIL ARROW

detail
reference
number

DETAIL DETAIL
1/4"=1'-0"

detail name

draw LINE
to suit

scale of detail

detail
reference
sheet no.

DETAIL TITLE BLOCK

Figure 14

INSERTING OTHER SYMBOLS

Over 300 of the most commonly used architectural drafting symbols have been included in the Turbo Designer symbol library. Specific identifying information can be added to each one of these symbols when they are added to a drawing, so that the item(s) that each symbol represents can be kept track of with ei:MicroSpec.

It is easy to add one of these symbols to a drawing. Simply pick the symbol from either the Tablet Menu or from one of the Symbol Library Screen Menus, point to where you want to insert the symbol on the drawing screen and, again, press the pick button. After you have entered the identifying information about that symbol, the symbol will be inserted into the drawing. See inserted symbols on **Figure 15.**

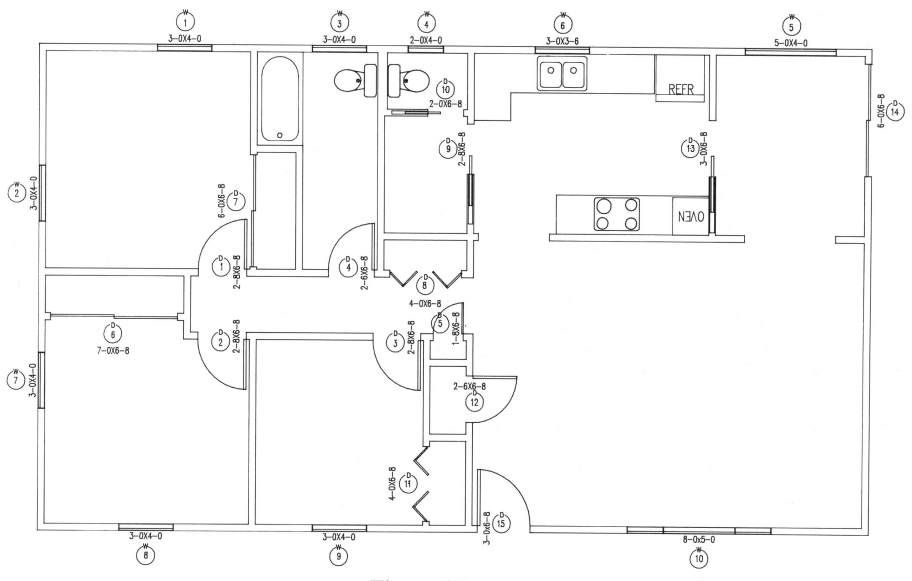

Figure 15

DRAWING ELECTRICAL PLANS

One of the big advantages of drafting with a computer is that you don't have to redraw your base plan everytime that you want to draw a different plan.

For example, here is how to draw an electrical plan on a previously developed floor plan. First, turn OFF all of the layers that aren't needed for an electrical plan such as dimensions, text and furniture. Next turn ON the layer that you will be drawing the electrical plan on and set the scale for the electrical plan (if it is to be a different scale from the base floor plan). Finally, draw the electrical plan (**Figure 16**).

At this point, you can either SAVE the electrical plan as a new drawing, or you can simply turn OFF the layer with the electrical symbols on it and continue with the original plans.

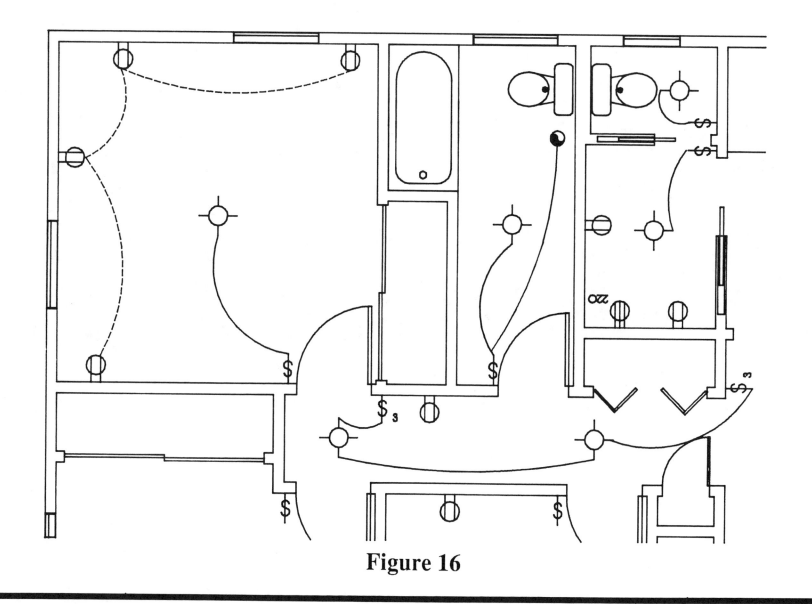

Figure 16

INTRODUCTION TO 3D CAD

Two-dimensional drafting systems have dominated the CAD marketplace, especially for the microcomputer user. With the advent of inexpensive plotters (starting in 1982), drafting applications became feasible. Although projections of three-dimensional objects can be prepared using 3D CAD, the demand for such projected images is not nearly as great as the demand for drafting-quality images. Change comes slowly, especially where fundamental changes in method are involved. Through the end of the eighties many applications will still depend on design methods which have changed little since the Egyptian architects drew on papyrus. The designer sketches a concept on paper. The sketches are delineated in the form of working drawings. Machinists take copies of those drawings (hopefully the latest revisions) and run machines which produce the final products.

The period from the early seventies through the mid-eighties will probably be remembered as one of transition from manual drafting to computer assisted drafting. If manual methods comprise the first phase (changing little over five thousand years), the second phase takes perhaps twenty years. The third phase is already upon us. Its origins are in the automotive and aerospace industries. Its chief characteristic is the direct use of machines to prepare the end product, without the use of drawings.

Where two-dimensional CAD won immediate acceptance in the drafting office, three-dimensional CAD has been harder to justify. Expensive hardware in the late sixties and through the seventies made it necessary to emphasize "drafting productivity" over modeling applications. Industry analysts estimated in the mid-seventies that three-dimensional applications accounted for merely five percent of total CAD use.

Yet the future will probably tell a completely different story. Paper drawings will be, especially in manufacturing, rapidly replaced by multi-dimensional models which are created and which remain resident in powerful computer systems. Most recently, affordable computer-driven machine tools are becoming available, making computer aided manufacturing accessible to small firms in much the same way that computer aided drafting has become feasible.

Existing three-dimensional systems are more difficult to typecast than are drafting systems. Many approaches have been and are being taken to the implementation of 3D CAD. The field is highly specialized, ranging from real-time simulations at the high end to "wireframe" modeling on the least expensive of microcomputers. It is this variety of applications that hints at the power which lies dormant in the 3D approach to design.

As the industrialized nations increasingly rely on robotics and other forms of factory automation, the three-dimensional system presents clearly superior capabilities compared to paper-oriented drafting systems. The manufacturing process is decidedly three-dimensional, dealing as it does with tangible volumetric objects. The trend, based on this new definition of productivity, is clearly away from paper drawings and toward simulation and direct machining. Microcomputers make computer aided manufacturing available on the factory floor.

Paper drawings, after all, involve a complex shorthand and consequent errors due to interpretation. To drive a machine directly and mill a part without the need for intermediate drawings is demonstrably more efficient and accurate. Future trends will be dramatically away from drafting and toward the "paperless factory." Such factories already exist to some extent and will increase in number. The transition will be dramatic because the savings can be achieved in many ways, as opposed to the relatively small benefits of automated drafting. For example, where the drafting application achieves efficiency through the automation of drawing, the automation of the manufacturing process itself achieves efficiency by eliminating the entire drafting function. But that's not all. Along with the savings achieved by circumventing drafting, other benefits accrue. Inventory can be automatically monitored. The design can be modified while it is being produced, on the factory floor, without the need to "redraw." Materials use can be more effectively controlled. The benefits are virtually unlimited.

As the neglected companion of mainframe drafting systems, 3D applications were seen as superfluous even after the cost of CAD was dramatically reduced by microcomputer hardware. Initial funding for 3D applications was extremely difficult to obtain because the investors tended to refer to early studies based on mainframe applications. Because there was less risk in implementing a drafting system, the investor was drawn to the two-dimensional approach. The trend toward this emphasis on "drawing productivity" extended well into the eighties.

ADD-ON 3D

Starting in 1985 a trend toward 3D began to become evident in the microcomputer CAD marketplace. Numerous small CAD systems were introduced emphasizing drafting features at low cost. But along with these systems, 3D was increasingly evident as "add-on" software for the already popular drafting systems. The very nature of a two-dimensional drafting system makes it difficult to treat 3D as an "add-on" feature. The "add-on" approach has been popular because it doesn't detract from the primary function of the drafting system. As far as being a useful implementation of 3D, however, the add-on falls short.

In the future, with manufacturing shifting toward total automation, investment goals will change from drafting applications to computer aided manufacturing (where the computer contols machine "islands") and then to computer *integrated* manufacturing (where the computer controls the entire manufacturing process). The time frame for the transition from drafting to integrated automation will be faster in certain industries than in others.

Traditionally, drafting has been prerequisite in such fields as architecture and civil engineering. These fields involve little or no direct manufacturing. Many intermediary disciplines will be involved. For example, the architect drafts a set of drawings which are examined by a contractor (and many subcontractors) and used by tradespeople to construct a building. It is hard to imagine that the need for drawings in this chain of events will decrease. On the other hand, the doors, windows and water closets that go into the completed structure will be increasingly manufactured by automated techniques. It is quite easy to see how drawings can be eliminated from the process of producing these component items.

COOPERS & LYBRAND "WALKTHRU" STORYBOARD

VARIETY OF 3D IMPLEMENTATIONS

Wireframe

What types of 3D CAD are available now? Perhaps the most numerous and inexpensive are the "wireframe" systems. A wireframe is, as its name suggests, a three-dimensional framework of lines. This type of system is easily implemented on a microcomputer because it requires little more than the ability to draw lines from one point in space to another, much as the drafting system draws lines on paper. To do much more tends to strain the resources of even the fastest conventional microcomputer. The wireframe system bridges the gap between drafting and modeling. If such a system is as good at drafting as it is at modeling (which is not often the case), it is light years ahead of the drafting-bound 2D system. The wireframe system is the core of most 3D applications which add other features. With it the user can specify the points in space which define volumes for later enhancement, even for processing by much more powerful computers.

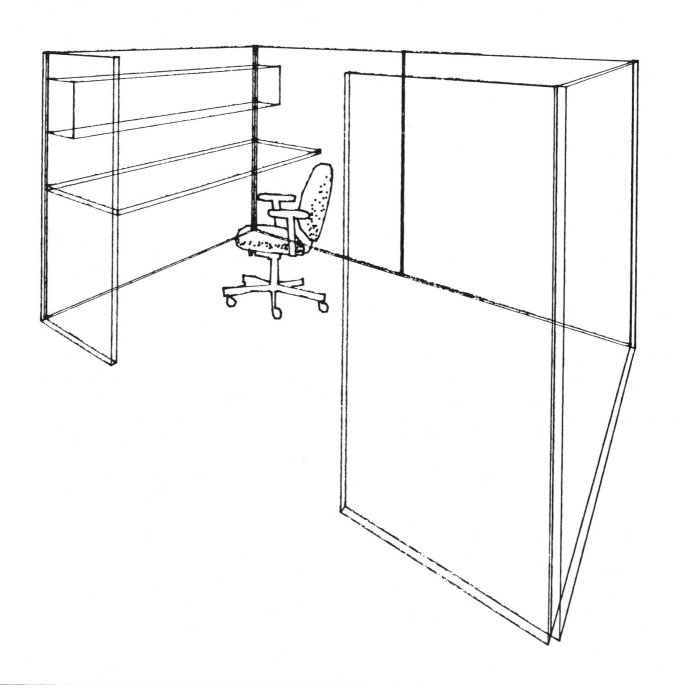

Hidden Line

At the next level of 3D implementation, lines in the wireframe model are removed (by a myriad of techniques) where they are hidden by user-defined plane surfaces. Hidden line removal (or occlusion) is achieved by highly sophisticated and complex algorithms (sequences of operations) which, because of their complexity, usually require hours and hours of processing time on microcomputers. Very few of these algorithms are defined well enough to guarantee successful occlusion under all circumstances. It is often impossible even to predict how long a given process of hidden line removal will take on the microcomputer. The human eye is often much more reliable and faster at removing hidden lines from perspective projections.

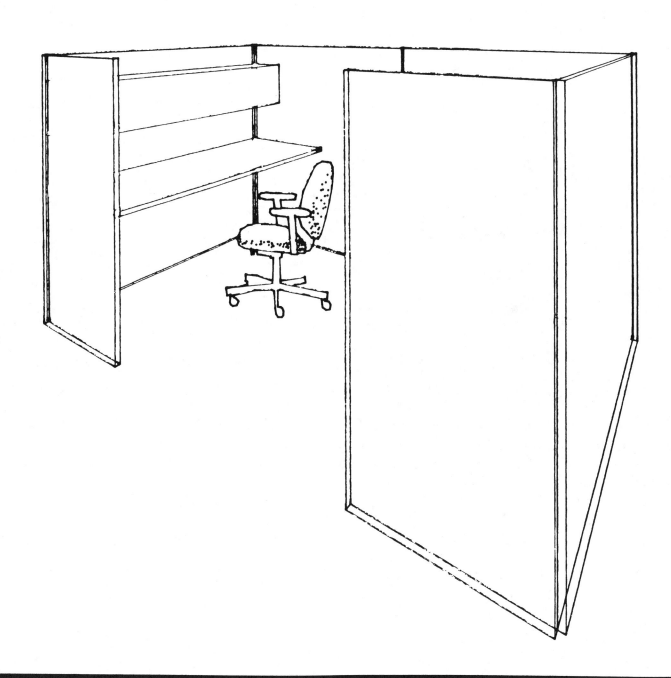

Extrusion

It is important to distinguish between "extrusion," or what is commonly called "two and a half" dimensional systems and "true" three-dimensional systems. One way to achieve the appearance of three-dimensional objects is to use the 2D data as a "floor" and "extrude" the vertical information artificially. This method is often adopted by drafting systems when they try to add 3D modeling capabilities. The information contained in such an extruded model consists of the X,Y locations of line endpoints in two dimensions and the height that these lines are to be elevated above the X,Y plane. This information does not include detailed coordinates for each line endpoint in space and hence is limited to constructions, such as in walls, where the plan information is merely repeated at a given height above the floor.

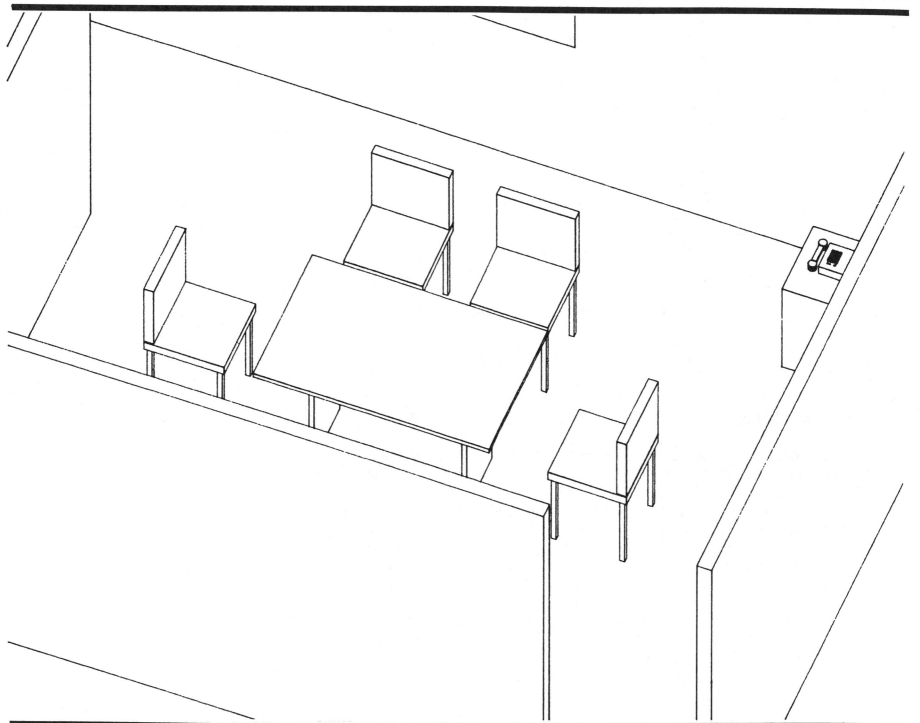

Surface Modeling

Beyond the wireframe world is the realm of surface modeling. Using this technique, the planes defined by edges drawn by lines are replaced by painted surfaces which lend a sense of solidity and reality to the computer generated object. Such surfaces can consist of solid, uniform colors, which can be shaded using synthetic light sources and given textures, transparency, reflectivity, translucency and a host of other properties. The sophistication of the surface modeling system is limited only by the cost of writing the complex code and the cost of the specialized high-speed hardware required. Surface modeling systems are useful in product visualization and presentation applications. Many of the exciting computer synthetic images on television use this level of technology. Real-time surface modeling is even possible with some specialized systems. The average microcomputer can perform some carefully limited surface modeling functions.

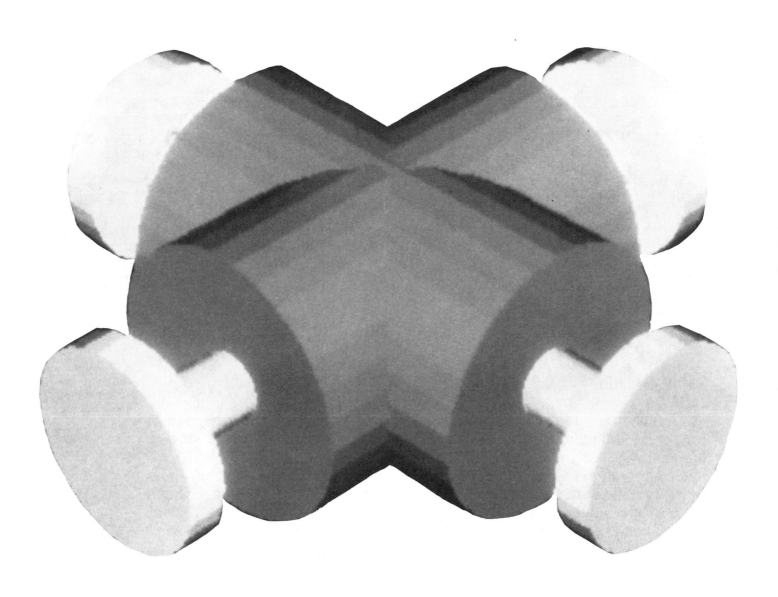

Solid Modeling

The highest level of 3D modeling is done by mainframe systems used for "solid modeling" such as analyzing oil deposits. Where the surface modeling system needs to keep track of information relating only to the outer skin of a volume, the solid modeling system keeps track of finite volumes which are combined to form the larger volume of the model. Such systems are valuable in analyzing oil deposits because each cubic foot of material can be represented, along with its properties of elasticity, porocity, and any other attribute we might wish to model. You can readily see that the amount of information available in such a system requires very high speed on the part of the computer. True solid modeling is usually done using the fastest mainframe computers costing millions of dollars.

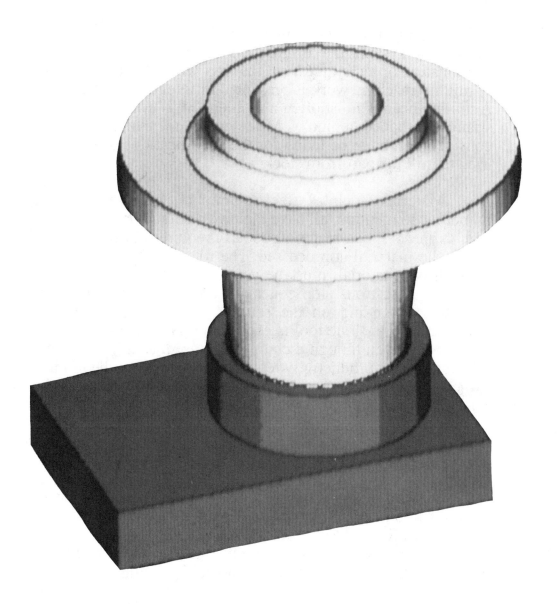

Manufacturing

Manufacturing systems are designed around the "tool pass" concept. In such a system the original model may have been evolved using a combination of techniques, but the data which is used to make a lathe, press or milling machine work is presented differently than with a drafting plotter. A milling head is most often a rotating "mill" which looks like a drill with a strangely shaped point. Mills come in many shapes and sizes, so consideration must be made for the specifications of the tool which will be used to mill the part from stock.

Materials such as steel, aluminum, brass, plastics, and others too numerous to mention, all have their own unique properties of ductility, mass, and hardness. Each material property requires allowances for the speed with which the material is processed. The rotation of the mill, as well as its path through the material, must be governed by the computer program used to drive it. Disastrous consequences can result, including hazards to the operator, depending on the settings of the machine with respect to the materials. A machine tool is considerably more complicated than a drafting plotter, and even though a computer is used, a skilled machinist is required. Where drafting productivity requires an operator skilled in the delineation of project requirements, machining productivity requires the skills of a machinist who is familiar with the materials to be worked.

3D SYSTEM DESIGN PRINCIPLES

A word about 3D system design. The effectiveness of a 3D system depends upon the *edit* function. Everything you do as you work with the system involves editing your model. You should be able to relocate any point (or node) in the 3D space without disturbing other parts of the model. There should be several different methods of doing the same thing, such as editing by search, location in space, or location in the database. Data used in the model should be accessible to other systems through the use of transport standards. Examples of such standards are Initial Graphics Exchange

Specification (IGES) and Virtual Device Interface/Computer Graphics Interface (VDI/CGI). The 3D system should enable you to work directly in a projection of the space occupied by the model. Many 3D systems only permit working on plan and elevation views of the model. You should be able to work in perspective, isometric, plan or elevation, and rotate the space and the objects within the space either as a whole or in part. You should be able to extract information concerning the objects that make up the model for use with software which tabulates information about the model.

One of the reasons 3D has been so hard to add to drafting software is that the editing process is much different with a 3D system. In a 2D system, for example, you never need to confront the problem of lines being drawn in space *above* other lines. To identify the line on the drawing is all you need to do to begin editing it. With a 3D system you need to identify which of several lines, some of which may overlap in whole or in part, are to be edited.

With the growing variety of 3D applications packages becoming available there should be something for everyone. One of the extremely encouraging aspects of 3D CAD is that there is an enormous richness and variety to it. In drafting applications it is possible to find systems that solve the drafting problem in a nearly generic way. In other words, there probably *can* be the world's best drafting system, but *not* the world's best 3D system. There's just too much variety among the problems that need to be solved.

3D FOR THE ARCHITECT

What can three-dimensional CAD do for the architect? To be successful, the architect must express three-dimensional concepts. Clients are often unable to visualize the appearance of a finished design given plan and elevation views. Traditionally, the solution to the problem of presentation has been the construction of models and the production of architectural renderings.

Three-dimensional CAD can assist the architect in preparing accurate projections of building designs. Because the 3D database can be made to simulate actual points in space, a simple process can be used to simulate the process of projection using an "artificial camera." The "artificial camera" creates more accurate projections than the use of shorthand methods (the "office method," for example) and also eliminates much of the drudgery involved in such projections.

Architectural models can be cut using automated machinery. Such hardware, although still expensive, is rapidly being made affordable. A typical price for desktop computer assisted machining is around $20,000, including all hardware and software.

The computer can also be used effectively to perform design studies which, because they are executed directly in space, automatically solve the "corner" conditions, where much effort is normally required to achieve accuracy. All too often the elevations do not accurately coincide with reality because they are developed separately. Using 3D CAD the designer is forced to think in spatial, rather than derived, terms.

The emphasis that has been placed on drafting functions has unfortunately obscured the value of working with a multi-dimensional database from the start of the project. With the low cost of present-day computers and the many uses to which they can be put, it is not difficult to justify the use of the computer in early studies.

Despite the early need to cost-justify the use of the computer by using it for "production," the trend now is more toward design and the 3D database. One problem resulting from this strange reversal of functions (the cart before the horse) is that the design process does not flow smoothly from design studies into the drafting of working drawings. There is no substantial reason to limit the use of the computer to drafting. Microcomputers justify themselves easily when used only for word processing. Every designer should use one, even if only to prepare project correspondence and specifications! In the business world this is certainly true.

The early purchasers of microcomputers, nevertheless, seem to have been motivated to justify their purchases by resorting to the reasoning that in order to offset the $5,000 to $10,000 cost it had to be put to work doing production drafting. The use of the computer to do design studies is often viewed as frivolous.

When the computer is *not* used to do design studies, however, the result is that the drafter needs to perform the work of translating the design sketches into drafted documents. If the design studies are done using the computer in 3D they can be "taken apart" and scaled to form the basis for drafting. This saves a lot of work and leads to drawings that are much more accurate. Most of the problems that arise from inaccurate correlations between plan and elevation views have already been solved.

Design studies include, for example, the tabulation of a myriad of design features. Desks and chairs need to be assigned to offices. The design is really a database which evolves and becomes more complex. Where 3D projections are extended to include data that describes what the design elements are, how much they cost, where they can be obtained, etc., the project benefits. The client sees what the proposed design "looks like" and how much it might cost, and the designer knows much more about the project as a whole.

When the design development phase terminates and the production of working drawings and specifications begins, access to such a comprehensive database can be invaluable. If only drafting is supported by the computer there is little gained, except perhaps for an economy which derives from the easy repetition of groups of lines.

It seems the initial romance of the computer is over, and the architect is now exploring new territory. Computers are such a new entry into an ancient profession that change is bound to happen slowly.

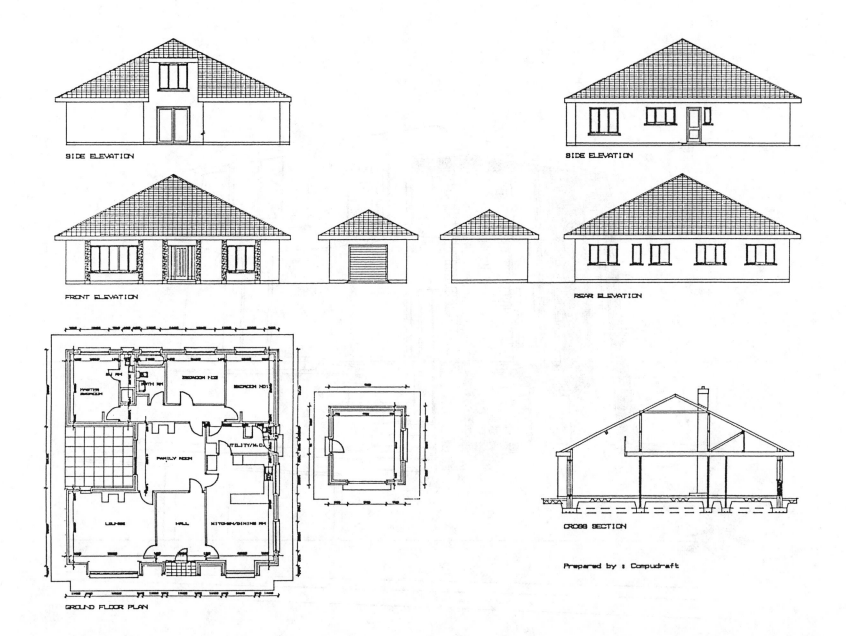

SIDE ELEVATION

SIDE ELEVATION

FRONT ELEVATION

REAR ELEVATION

GROUND FLOOR PLAN

CROSS SECTION

Prepared by : Compudraft

ONE POINT PERSPECTIVE

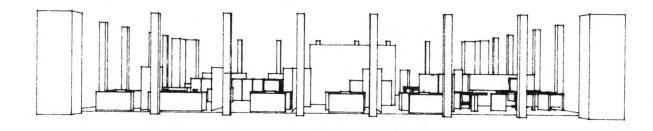

TWO POINT PERSPECTIVE

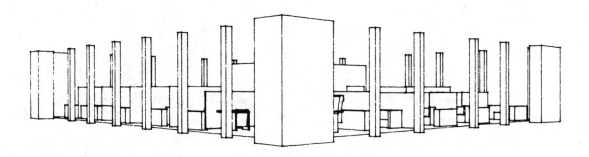

THREE POINT PERSPECTIVE

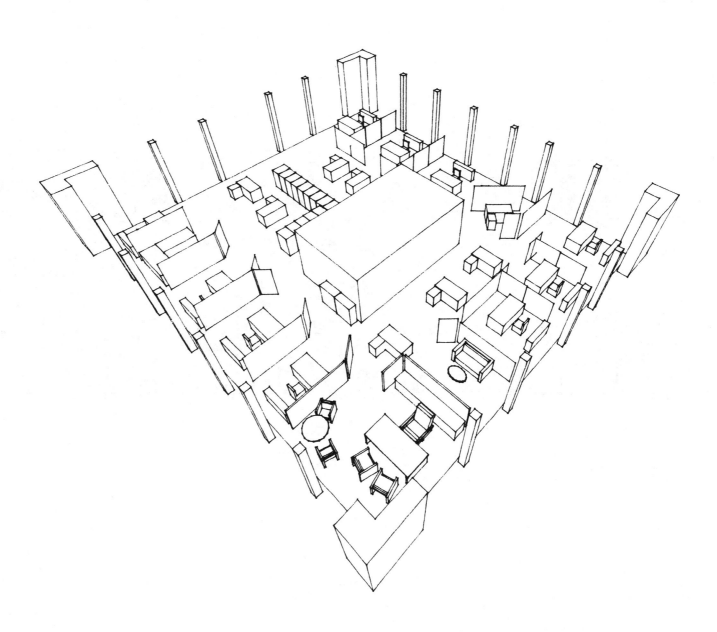

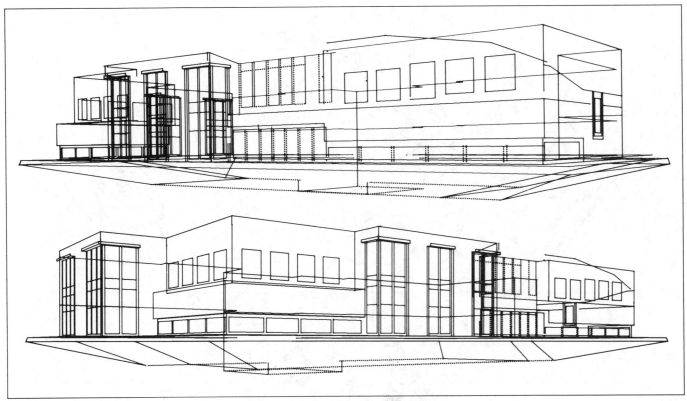

Potter, Lawson & Pawlowsky produced these drawings after just 20 hours of experience with MicroCAD. They are early perspectives for an office building currently under construction in suburban Madison, Wis.

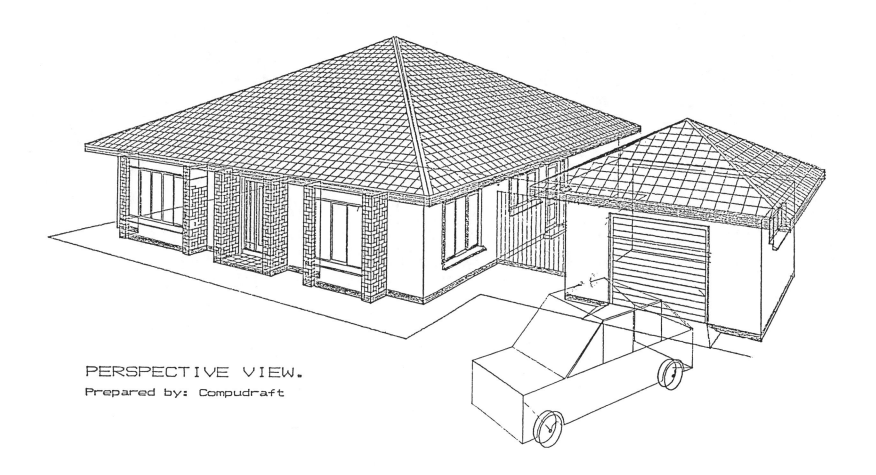

PERSPECTIVE VIEW.

Prepared by: Compudraft

6. SPECIFICATIONS

Specifications are the other half of construction documents that are not represented by drawings or graphics. They are the written and mathematical data which more fully describe the project and its development, products and process.

Specifications can include bills-of-materials, building code data, costs, installation instructions, contract provisions or other descriptions. The format of construction specifications may conform to the guidelines of the American Institute of Architects (A.I.A.) and be based on the standard "boiler-plate" specifications published as MasterSpec™, or they may conform to the related guidelines promulgated by the Construction Specification Institute (C.S.I.).

The principal way in which the designer can automate the specification development process with the microcomputer is by using word processing and database programs either by themselves or linked with the CAD system. MasterSpec is basically a database of word processing standard paragraphs and sections for the designer to select from and edit into a custom document. Database programs such as dBase III™ allow the designer to customize information such as bills-of-materials and include them into the specifications.

Specific application software such as ei:MicroSpec integrates and manages the entire specification process including the connections with CAD, database managers, word processing and MasterSpec. In this chapter I will introduce the reader to ei:MicroSpec and describe how specifications can be developed with this system.

ei:MicroSpec helps the architect, engineer and designer develop and manage the specification and administration of materials, services and products. ei:MicroSpec is a computer aided specifying system and integrates with computer aided drafting systems like AutoCAD, Cadvance and VersaCAD, thereby automating the entire design process. ei:MicroSpec firmly establishes the concept of computer integrated design.

HOW ei:MICROSPEC FITS IN

The three primary elements of contract document development consume varying percentages of the project's resources. In the typical facilities design project 30% of the designer's resources is spent on drawings, 50% on the selection and specification of products and materials, and 20% on logistic management and scheduling. Using this premise, ei:MicroSpec addresses 70% of the design process and CAD graphics only 30%. This means that for many design offices, ei:MicroSpec is more central than CAD by itself. This ratio, of course, varies by discipline and project.

Increased Productivity

The traditional argument for CAD is based on increased production, ease of revision and decreased errors and ommissions. However, this leaves the area of specification and administration of materials unaddressed. A more significant advantage occurs when CAD and programs like ei:MicroSpec are integrated. Written specifications, job costing and project management are developed simultaneously and automatically as products and materials are inserted into the design drawing. In actual use, productivity increase realized with CAD alone rarely exceeds two times manual output. With automated specifications this efficiency can be magnified to a much greater extent. Furthermore, the earliest design becomes the skeleton of the following stage and so on, without redrawing and revision.

Enhanced Quality

Productivity increases alone are not the only justification for using the computer in your document production. The tedious job of developing project specifications is greatly relieved, allowing the designer or project manager to focus on the design development or management process. Many more design alternatives become possible, more time to spend checking and evaluating delivery and pricing strategies is allowed, and a greater percentage of the project time can be allotted to client development. This reallocation of resources can increase client communication and design quality, and open new possibilities to provide additional services. Best of all, you can be free to express your creativity the way you have dreamed of since deciding to enter the design profession.

New Services to Offer

The ever increasing competition in the business of design and architecture combined with dwindling profits make it important to find new and unique services to offer your clients. These services can become both new profit centers and ways to differentiate yourself from the rest of the pack. Computer aided design can allow you to offer extensive facilities management services that continue beyond the installation phase. Maintaining product inventory and reallocating resources can give you an inside edge on future business and, at the same time, bring in additional revenues. Cost studies and product evaluations become feasible with the ei:MicroSpec system. A renewed emphasis on the design process is possible inside edge on future business and, at the same time, bring in additional revenues. Cost studies and product evaluations become feasible with the ei:MicroSpec system. A renewed emphasis on the design process is possible when the cost of contract documents can be proportionally decreased. The possibilities are limitless!

How Does It Work?

ei:MicroSpec uses an easy-to-learn system of menus and windows to select, integrate and transfer data between your own choices of CAD, accounting and word processing programs. One important aspect of ei:MicroSpec is its integration with AutoCAD, Cadvance, VersaCAD, MicroCAD and other popular CAD packages. The system begins a project at the preliminary design stage with an outline specification. It allows the designer to specify, document and track product information, accumulating all bill-of-materials and project management information until bidding or automatic generation with the full accounting systems.

ei:MicroSpec allows the user to develop extensive databases of items such as furniture, wallcovering, lighting fixtures and mechanical parts, and then to assemble them into categories such as rooms, buildings, subsystems, facilities or interiors specification. The final product can be generated as bid documents, bills-of-materials or purchase orders, and can merge with word processing databases such as MasterSpec. The specification database may be automatically transformed into an assets management and inventory system for your company or client.

ei:MicroSpec features an electronic catalogue which provides automated product selection, information and pricing for anything from lighting fixtures to furnishings. While the catalogues are easily created by the user, predefined catalogues for Herman Miller, Steelcase and other manufacturers are available along with selected CAD symbol libraries.

ei:MICROSPEC AND SPECIFICATIONS

When you are setting up a project on ei:MicroSpec, you have to organize your procedures and thinking. The process, however, is very similar to the one you are accustomed to using. This necessary organization is a real asset of the system, as it helps you with in-depth project management, including documentation of contacts with suppliers, records of revisions, and versions of your specifications and proposals. It also allows you to easily update documents that otherwise might be avoided because of time constraints.

First, you need to define all of the companies you will be using in the project, and then enter them into the Company file using the Company Maintenance routine. These companies should include your clients, supplier, vendors, manufacturers, and in fact anyone you might refer to in the Item Prefix Company Code or Vendor Code fields of the entry screen.

```
06/04/85                        ei:MicroSpec                         V-1.0
                        ══ Eclat Infomedia, Inc. ══
                           Company Maintenance
  ┌────────────────────────────────────────────────────────────────────┐
  │ ┌──────────────────────────────────────────────────────────────┐   │
  │ │                                                                │   │
  │ │     Company Code    EI                                         │   │
  │ │                                                                │   │
  │ │     Company Name    ECLAT INFOMEDIA, INC.                      │   │
  │ │                                                                │   │
  │ │     Co. Address 1   38660 LEXINGTON ST., SUITE #454            │   │
  │ │                                                                │   │
  │ │     Co. Address 2                                              │   │
  │ │                                                                │   │
  │ │     City/St/Zip     FREMONT              CA    94536-          │   │
  │ │                                                                │   │
  │ │     Contact         FREDERIC H. JONES, PRESIDENT               │   │
  │ │                                                                │   │
  │ │     Phone           (415) 794-6925                             │   │
  │ │                                                                │   │
  │ │     Comment         CALL FROM 9 'TILL 5.                       │   │
  │ │                                                                │   │
  │ └──────────────────────────────────────────────────────────────┘   │
  └────────────────────────────────────────────────────────────────────┘

                   Please enter Company information.
```

This file is provided to ease the monotonous entry of the company information by the data operator. It also enables the entering to be much more accurate and consistent. Finally, it provides the basis for purchase order generation information as well as automated vendor list creation to accompany your specification documents.

The only information in the Company file essential to other data files is the Company Code. The Company Code corresponds to the Item and Assembly Prefix as well as the Category Company Codes. It can be looked at as the project designator in this instance, and all files for a single project should use the same convention, i.e.: ABC, ABC-O-CH1. This will enable your data to be easily grouped by project within the system, and will facilitate the discrimination of one project from another in reports. As always, if you add new companies to the project later, you can add them to the Company file.

The next file to set up is the Catalogue. This module is optional in project use and can be used for some items and not for others. For example, you can maintain a Herman Miller catalogue in the system and call information out of it for item definitions at item entry time. Unique products that are specified infrequently, and which would clutter up the catalogue file, may be added directly into the Item file.

The catalogue may be established by your own staff, or many contract furniture and architectural specialties catalogue modules are available from manufacturers. If you are using large blocks of repetitive products in a project, this can be a very powerful tool and can eliminate costly catalogue misinformation and incorrect pricing in specifications and proposals.

```
06/04/85                          ei:MicroSpec                          V-1.0
                           ═══ Eclat Infomedia, Inc. ═══
                               Catalogue Maintenance
 ┌───────────────────────────────────────────────────────────────────────┐
 │                                                                         │
 │        Catalogue No.  AO884 FFMT                                        │
 │                                                                         │
 │        Company Code   HM                                                │
 │                                                                         │
 │        Vendor         Herman Miller, Inc.                               │
 │                                                                         │
 │        Catalogue Pg.  14                                                │
 │                                                                         │
 │        Description    Panel, 62 x 24                                    │
 │                                                                         │
 │        Shipping Wt.    87.00                                            │
 │                                                                         │
 │        Unit of Meas.  EA                                                │
 │                                                                         │
 │        Unit Price      370.00                                           │
 │                                                                         │
 └───────────────────────────────────────────────────────────────────────┘
 <W>rite to file, <M>odify data, <F>wd, <B>ack, or <Q>uit?  (W/M/F/B/Q) ==>
```

The third step in project establishment is the selection of items for your palette. This is one of the most important concepts of the ei:MicroSpec system. Every project must have the items that are used in it defined as items. They must then be assigned an item code with prefix, status code and tag code.

```
PREFIX  STATUS  TAG CODE
   |       |       |
 ABC─┤O├─CH1
```

The prefix assigns the item to a specific project and should conform with the code assigned to the project in the company file. ABC might be <ABC> corporation or AlphaBeta Corporation Project "C." This prefix should be consistent for all items assigned to a specific project, so that the items for that project can be segregated and called up in an organized fashion. If you wish to import items from another project, a new prefix, status and/or tag code must be assigned with the item status change utility or <C>opy command.

The status code is a method of discriminating between multiple levels of identical or similar items, or between items with different dispositions. Examples might be "O" for items that are "on order," or "I" for "installed." When taking inventory of existing items, the status codes might stand for "G" (good condition), "F" (fair condition), or any other designation you find useful. There are many places in reports where the item code is called on to sort for a particular group of items. It is recommended that your company standardize all the system codes so that shared data are consistent.

```
06/04/85                          ei:MicroSpec                        V-1.0
                            ═ Eclat Infomedia, Inc. ═
                                Item Maintenance

  Item #      ABC-O-CH1        Co. HM  Catalog # AO4321
                                                                    Pg 23
  Vendor      Herman Miller
  Descrip     Executive Swivel Chair
  Size        NA
  Cover       #321 Hopsack, Blue
  Finish      Putty
  Misc1       Hard Casters
  Misc2       NA
  Source      ABC ABC CORPORATION
  Delivery    ASAP                                      Ship Wt.      43.00
  CAD Count        0.00          CSI # NA

  Quote       Bill Smith        Quote Date 09/09/85     Rev. Date    / /

  On Hand           3.00  UM EA  List Pr.   450.00  PC B  Unit Pr.   270.00


 # not found.   <R>eenter, <D>sply #'s, <A>ccept #, or <Q>uit?  (R/D/A/Q) ==>
```

The final step has two branches that assemble the items into groups: the Assembly, which gathers together groups of items, and the Category, which may group both items and assemblies.

The assembly has a code identical to the item code.

PREFIX STATUS TAG CODE

ABC-O-CH1F

The assembly also has a description field in its header and carries the value of the accumulated total values of the items assigned to it. An example of an assembly could be a workstation made up of many individual parts which have been previously defined as items.

The utility of the assembly module is to create a single entry of individual parts that would generally be thought of as a group or sub-assembly in the overall project. Other examples might include electronic sub-assemblies, HVAC zones or furniture systems.

```
06/04/85                         ei:MicroSpec                        ▼-1.0
                          = Eclat Infomedia, Inc. =
                              Assembly Maintenance

  Assembly #  ABC-O-TEST

  Company     ABC CORPORATION

  Descrip     Workstation 1              UM EA   Unit Price     384.00


   Item #   ABC-O-Cl            Descrip    CONNETOR, 2 WAY 90 CORNER

   UM EA    Quantity    8.00    List Price    80.00

            CAD Count   0.00    Unit Price    48.00    Total     384.00


 ** START **   <C>py, <M>od, <A>dd, <D>el, <F>wd, or <Q>uit? (C/M/A/D/F/Q) =>
```

The category is the primary grouping of items and assemblies and constitutes the basis of many of the most important system reports. A category can represent a room, e.g., "Bill Smith's Office" or "Room 101," and within a category you might assign items that represent chairs and desks, or an assembly that represents a work station or a set of modular furniture. The category is identified by a company code that is similar to the item and assembly prefix in that it groups the category by project. The category is then further defined by the category number which might consist of, for example, "Room 110," and two further defining fields initialized by the system as location and description. Location, which can be user-defined in the installation routine, might be a physical location, e.g. "Building A" or "100 Main Street" and description might be "Bill Smith's Office," "drafting area," or "mechanical system."

To reiterate the project set-up process:

1. Assign company codes in the company maintenance routine to all projects, vendors, suppliers, etc.

2. Enter and catalogue data that you wish to use in the project into the catalogue file.

3. Define as many items for your project as you can initially, understanding that you can continually modify existing items, or add new items as you go along.

4. Define any assemblies that you wish to carry into category files.

5. Assign all project and assemblies to appropriate categories.

This is only a suggested process, and there are many alternative processes and variations possible with a system as flexible as ei:MicroSpec.

```
06/04/85                        ei:MicroSpec                        V-1.0
                        ═══ Eclat Infomedia, Inc. ═══
                             Category Maintenance

   Co.  ABC     ABC CORPORATION                         Category  101

   Place       Building A

   Descrip     Joe Jones' Office


   Item #    ABC-O-CH1          I/A I   Descrip Executive Swivel Chair

   UM EA     Quantity    2.00    List Price    450.00

             CAD Count   0.00    Unit Price    270.00    Total      540.00

  ** START **   <C>py, <M>od, <A>dd, <D>el, <F>wd, or <Q>uit? (C/M/A/D/F/Q) =>
```

FLOW DIAGRAM

This flow diagram shows the relationships between ei:MicroSpec and its various modules and external programs such as 2D and 3D CAD, word processing and accounting.

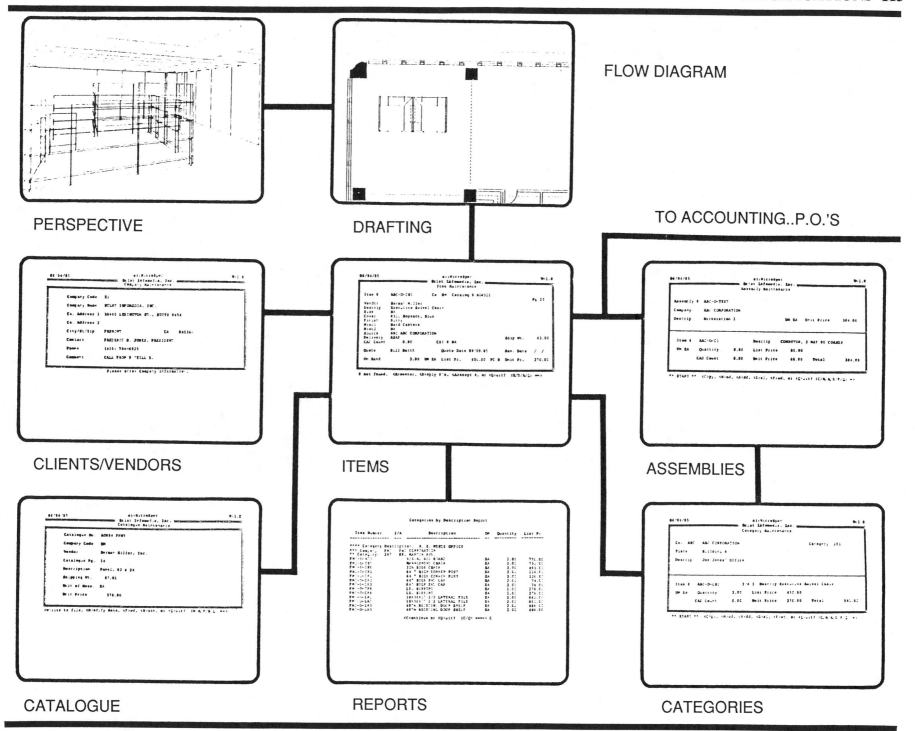

PERSPECTIVE

DRAFTING

FLOW DIAGRAM

TO ACCOUNTING..P.O.'S

CLIENTS/VENDORS

ITEMS

ASSEMBLIES

CATALOGUE

REPORTS

CATEGORIES

DESIGN

The design can be developed using the 3D CAD system linked to ei:MicroSpec. This will allow initial bills-of-materials and project costing to be done very early in the process. These drawings and schedules can then become templates for 2D drafting and specifications.

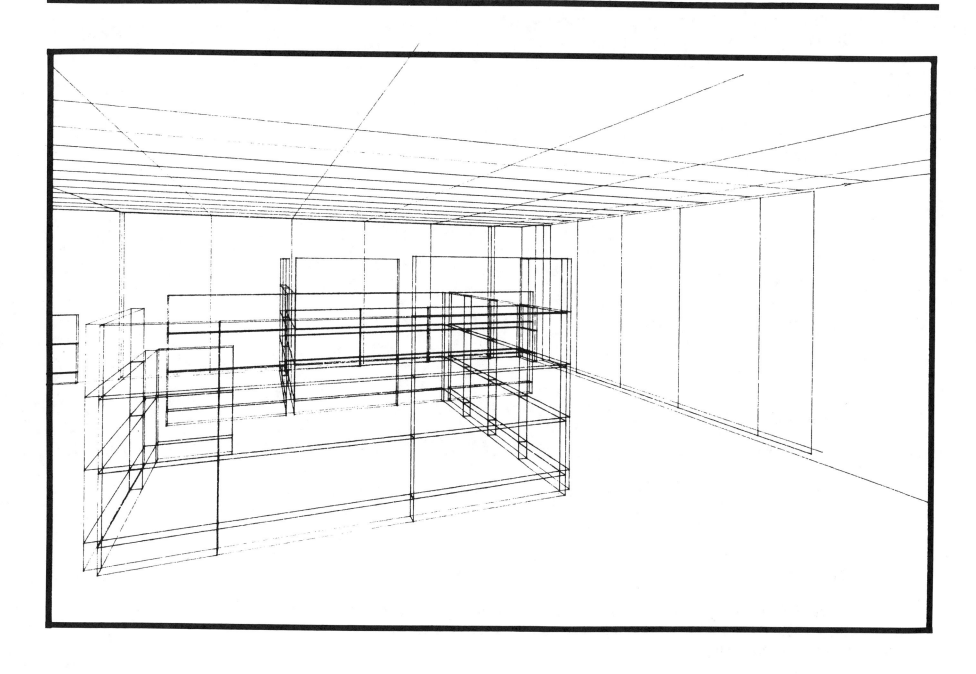

PRESENTATION

The design drawing can be rendered to form the basis for presentation to the client. The earlier wireframe image in this case was used as the basis for a quick pencil rendering.

Nelson Johnson, AIA

INSTALLATION PLAN

In developing your project with a CAD system, each item specified is assigned a symbol (or vice versa, depending on how you are developing the design).   A symbol can represent a piece of furniture, connector, light fixture, door, window, etc. When you move or edit the symbol, the related data in ei:MicroSpec is updated accordingly.

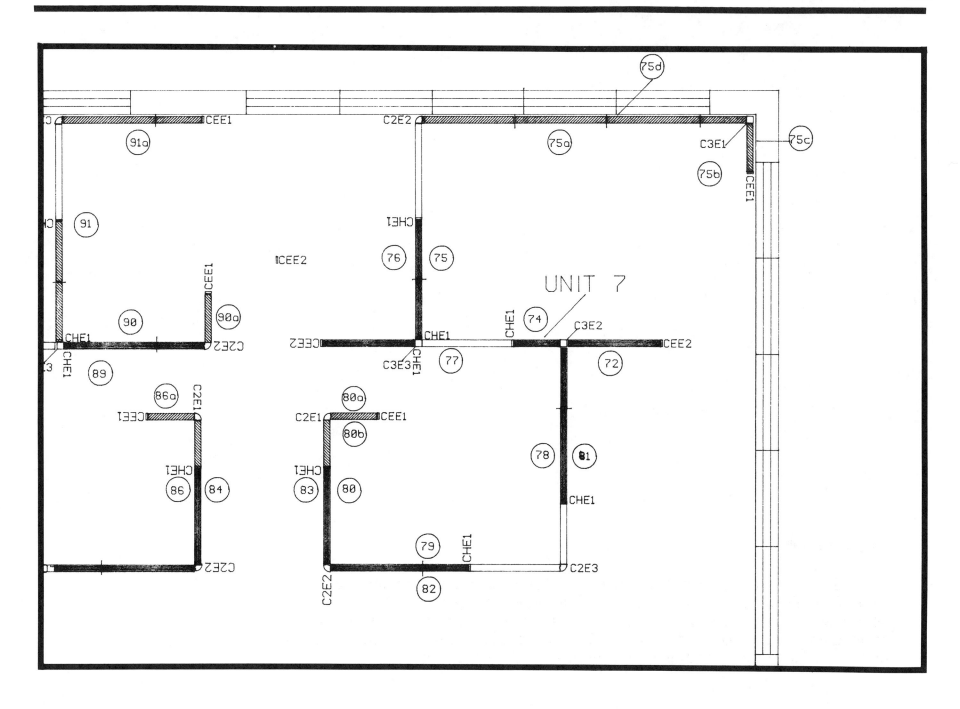

ELEVATIONS

Symbols are not restricted to plans. Elevation can represent items as well. The elevations shown on the opposite page are symbols of Herman Miller Ethospace™ tiles, which can be specified and counted in elevation more appropriately than plan. The 3D drawing can also contain symbols as in the wireframe representation of this installation shown earlier.

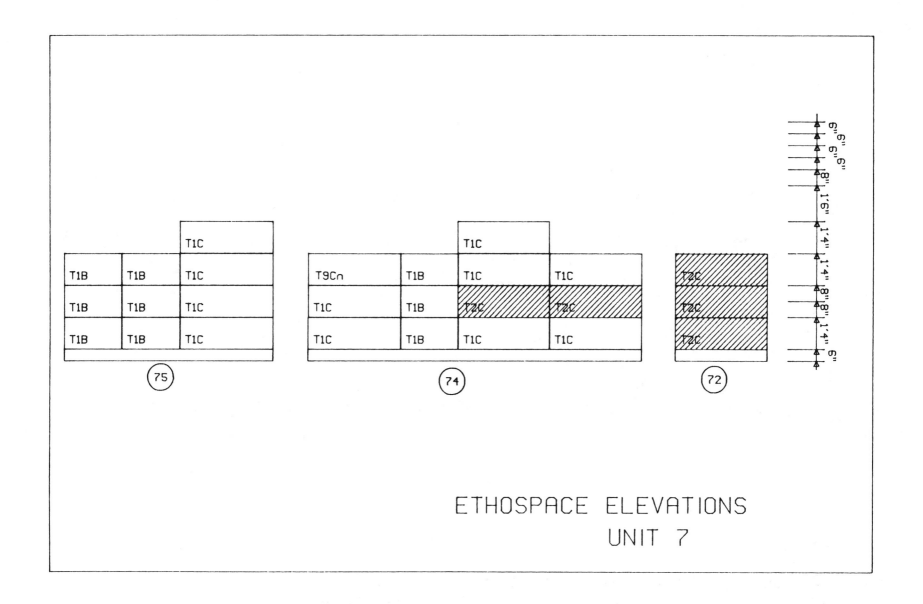

ETHOSPACE ELEVATIONS
UNIT 7

SYMBOLS

The page of Ethospace symbols shown here represents the library of symbols from which the elevation and plan symbols shown in the installation and elevaton drawings were selected.

E311024E		E311030E		E311048E	
E311024P		E311030P		E311048P	
E312024E		E312030E		E312048E	
E312024P		E312030P		E312048P	
E313024E		E313030E		E313048E	
E313224E		E313230E		E313248E	
E314024E		E314030E		E314048E	
E314124E		E314130E		E314148E	
E314224E		E314230E		E314248E	

ETHOSPACE SYMBOL LIBRARY

MASTER ITEM LIST

The master item list is the basic index of every product specified in your project. Both cost and project administration/scheduling information can be printed. This document is the major control document from the design, through bidding, to installation.

```
                           Eclat Infomedia, Inc.


           Page No.      1
           01/13/86


                        Master Item List for NEXT INCORPORATED

           ================================================================

           ITEM NUMBER:  NXT-0-C2E1
           CATALOG NO.:  E1220 38 HF
           VENDOR NAME:  HERMAN MILLER
           ITEM DESC. :  TWO-WAY 90 DEGREE CONNECTOR
           SIZE       :  38" HIGH
           COVER      :  NA
           FINISH     :  HF
           MISC1      :  NA
           MISC2      :  NA
           SOURCE     :  NOT APPLICABLE
           DELIVERY   :  ASAP
           CAD COUNT  :  2.00
           ON HAND    :  0.00
           UNIT MEAS. :  EA
           UNIT PRICE :  69.00          QTY: 1.00          TOTAL:  69.00


           ITEM NUMBER:  NXT-0-C2E2
           CATALOG NO.:  E1220 54 HF
           VENDOR NAME:  HERMAN MILLER
           ITEM DESC. :  TWO-WAY 90 DEGREE CONNECTOR
           SIZE       :  54" HIGH
           COVER      :  NA
           FINISH     :  HF
           MISC1      :  NA
           MISC2      :  NA
           SOURCE     :  NOT APPLICABLE
           DELIVERY   :  ASAP
           CAD COUNT  :  2.00
           ON HAND    :  0.00
           UNIT MEAS. :  EA
           UNIT PRICE :  80.00          QTY: 1.00          TOTAL:  80.00


           ITEM NUMBER:  NXT-0-C2E3
           CATALOG NO.:  E1220 70 HF
           VENDOR NAME:  HERMAN MILLER
           ITEM DESC. :  TWO-WAY 90 DEGREE CONNECTOR
           SIZE       :  70" HIGH
           COVER      :  NA
           FINISH     :  HF
           MISC1      :  NA
           MISC2      :  NA
           SOURCE     :  NOT APPLICABLE
           DELIVERY   :
           CAD COUNT  :  4.00
           ON HAND    :  0.00
           UNIT MEAS. :  EA
           UNIT PRICE :  88.00          QTY: 2.00          TOTAL:  176.00
```

MASTER CATEGORY LIST

Each category and assembly of items selected in a project has a related print-out. The print-out includes the quantities of items and assemblies assigned to each category, as well as description and pricing. These reports allow not only a detailed representation of the project but clear cost analysis of budget distribution. Custom reports for projects are easily generated.

```
                        Eclat Infomedia, Inc.


        Page No.      4
        01/13/86

                    Master Category List for NEXT INCORPORATED

        ==========================================================================


        ITEM NUMBER   :  NXT-0-T2C
        DESCRIPTION   :  BELTLINE WIRE MANAGEMENT TILE
        CAD COUNT     :        7.00
        QUANTITY USED:         7.00
        UNIT MEASURE  :  EA
        SELLING PRICE:        82.00           ITEM TOTAL:            574.00

        ITEM NUMBER   :  NXT-0-T4A
        DESCRIPTION   :  FACE TILE
        CAD COUNT     :        4.00
        QUANTITY USED:         4.00
        UNIT MEASURE  :  EA
        SELLING PRICE:        38.00           ITEM TOTAL:            152.00

        ITEM NUMBER   :  NXT-0-T4C
        DESCRIPTION   :  FACE TILE
        CAD COUNT     :        2.00
        QUANTITY USED:         2.00
        UNIT MEASURE  :  EA
        SELLING PRICE:        58.00           ITEM TOTAL:            116.00

        ITEM NUMBER   :  NXT-0-T9CN
        DESCRIPTION   :  TACKABLE TILE
        CAD COUNT     :        4.00
        QUANTITY USED:         4.00
        UNIT MEASURE  :  EA
        SELLING PRICE:        58.00           ITEM TOTAL:            232.00

                                    ** CATEGORY TOTAL:           10,095.00

                                   *** COMPANY TOTAL:            10,095.00

                                             6.5% TAX:              656.17

                                 ***** GRAND TOTAL:             10,751.17
```

HARDWARE SPECIFICATIONS

The hardware specification shown is only an example of the kind of documents possible when ei:MicroSpec is integrated with word processing databases such as MasterSpec or boilerplate generated directly by the designer. The computer manages and automatically assembles the complete specification document including schedules, costing and quantity information and legal and descriptive information.

```
====================================================================
                          SECTION 08710

                         FINISH HARDWARE
====================================================================
                        PART 1 - GENERAL

1.01 WORK INCLUDED
     A. Work under this section shall conform to the requirements
     in the xxxx Project Manual dated xxxxxxx.

     B.  The  following requirements shall supplement the Project
     manual.  Where conflicts occur, these current specifications
     shall govern.

                        PART 2 - PRODUCTS

2.01 HARDWARE
     A. Provide hardware groups as follows:

               DOOR HARDWARE GROUPS FOR ABC CORPORATION

** Assembly #:   HW-GROUP1
 * Description:  DOOR HARDWARE GROUP 1
------------------------------------------------------------------

ITEM NUMBER   :  ABC-S-HW1
DESCRIPTION   :  HINGES, ENTRANCE DOOR
CAD COUNT     :  0.00
QUANTITY USED:   1.00
UNIT MEASURE  :  PR
LIST PRICE    :  23.00              ITEM TOTAL:            23.00


ITEM NUMBER   :  ABC-S-HW2
DESCRIPTION   :  LATCHSET
CAD COUNT     :  0.00
QUANTITY USED:   1.00
UNIT MEASURE  :  EA
LIST PRICE    :  43.00              ITEM TOTAL:            43.00


ITEM NUMBER   :  ABC-S-HW3
DESCRIPTION   :  COAT HOOK
CAD COUNT     :  0.00
QUANTITY USED:   1.00
UNIT MEASURE  :  EA
LIST PRICE    :  14.00              ITEM TOTAL:            14.00


ITEM NUMBER   :  ABC-S-HW4
DESCRIPTION   :  FLOOR STOP
CAD COUNT     :  0.00
QUANTITY USED:   1.00
UNIT MEASURE  :  EA
LIST PRICE    :  18.50              ITEM TOTAL:            18.50

                               ** ASSEMBLY TOTAL:          98.50


                                1
```

HARDWARE SCHEDULE

Items can be grouped automatically by class. These reports can become Door, Window, Finish, Hardware and other schedules. The format can be as shown or the more traditional horizontal matrix can be used. The resulting schedule can be printed and bound into the project book, or can be read into the CAD drawing and plotted on sheets. They could also be printed on sticky-back acetate and applied to traditional tracings.

```
                        Eclat Infomedia, Inc.

Page No.       1
02/02/86

                HARDWARE SCHEDULE FOR ABC CORPORATION

===============================================================================


     ITEM NUMBER:  ABC-S-HW1
     CATALOG NO.:  1279L2
     VENDOR NAME:  HAGER
     ITEM DESC. :  HINGES, ENTRANCE DOOR
     TYPE       :  BACK FLAPS, TIGHT PIN
     FINISH     :  US10B
     MISC3      :  NA
     MISC4      :  NA
     MISC5      :  NA
     SOURCE     :  NOT APPLICABLE
     QUOTE      :  IMMEDIATELY AVAILABLE
     QUOTE      :  BILL SMITH
     DELIVERY   :  04/15/86
     REV. DATE  :    / /
     CAD COUNT  :  12.00
     ON HAND    :  0.00
     UNIT MEAS. :  PR
     LIST PRICE :  23.00




     ITEM NUMBER:  ABC-S-HW2
     CATALOG NO.:  M2100
     VENDOR NAME:  FALCON
     ITEM DESC. :  LATCHSET
     TYPE       :  VEGA-GALA
     FINISH     :  US12
     MISC3      :  NA
     MISC4      :  NA
     MISC5      :  NA
     SOURCE     :  NOT APPLICABLE
     QUOTE      :  IMMEDIATELY AVAILABLE
     QUOTE      :  BILL SMITH
     DELIVERY   :  04/15/86
     REV. DATE  :    / /
     CAD COUNT  :  12.00
     ON HAND    :  0.00
     UNIT MEAS. :  EA
     LIST PRICE :  43.00


                             1
```

PURCHASE ORDER

The ei:MicroSpec system allows the automatic generation of purchase orders for items specified. The computer accumulates all the items, their quantities and sources, and purchase orders are printed. The system can then pass the resulting data on to a complete accounting system.

```
Page No.    9
10/06/85


PURCHASE ORDER NUMBER:  TEST1234
```

```
                                          Ship To:

HERMAN MILLER                             ABC CORPORATION
8500 BYRON ROAD                           100 MAIN STREET
                                          SUITE 100
ZEELAND,  MI 49464                        ANYTOWN,  CA 12345
```

```
Item Number  :  ABC-O-WS2
Catalogue No.:  E2120 2472
Description  :  WORK SURFACE, VENEER
Size         :  24" X 72" LONG MITERED RIGHT
Cover        :  N/A
Finish       :  RA LIGHT ASH
Misc1        :  HF INNER TONE LIGHT
Misc2        :  N/A
Quantity     :       2.00     Unit Pr:     260.10     Total:        520.20
```

```
                                                  Page Total:        520.20
```

```
   Total Shipping Weight:     0.00        Grand Total:     6,117.30

   SHIP BY BEST METHOD......
   TAG ALL PJRODUCT WITH PURCHASE ORDER ITEM NUMBERS......
```

MASTER COMPANY LIST

The Master Company List is the accumulation of all the vendors whose products have been specified in the current project. This document is the Vendor List which accompanies a bid document.

```
                          Eclat Infomedia, Inc.

        Page No.       1
        10/06/85

                  Master Company List for ABC CORPORATION

        =====================================================================


        CO. NAME :   ABC CORPORATION
        CO. CODE :   ABC
        ADDRESS 1:   100 MAIN STREET
        ADDRESS 2:   SUITE 100
        CITY     :   ANYTOWN
        STATE    :   CA
        ZIP      :   12345
        CONTACT  :
        PHONE    :
        COMMENT  :


        CO. NAME :   DESIGN PERFORMANCE, INC.
        CO. CODE :   DP
        ADDRESS 1:   34 WEST SANTA CLARA STREET
        ADDRESS 2:   P.O. BOX 999
        CITY     :   SAN JOSE
        STATE    :   CA
        ZIP      :   95113
        CONTACT  :   JERRY ALLEN
        PHONE    :   (408) 288-7833
        COMMENT  :   BEST SALESMAN IN CALIFORNIA!!!!!!!!!!!!!


        CO. NAME :   HERMAN MILLER
        CO. CODE :   HM
        ADDRESS 1:   8500 BYRON ROAD
        ADDRESS 2:
        CITY     :   ZEELAND
        STATE    :   MI
        ZIP      :   49464
        CONTACT  :
        PHONE    :
        COMMENT  :
```

ITEMS BY DESCRIPTION

This is one of the many query reports possible to generate. Other reports might include move-in lists, department cost estimates, reports by item type or status, etc.

Eclat Infomedia, Inc.

Page No.   1
10/06/85

Items by Description Report for Prefix ABC

Item Number	Vendor	List Pr
----------------	---	---------

** Description: CHANGE OF HEIGHT FINISHED END
ABC-O-C4   HM   HERMAN MILLER   10.00

** Description: CONNECTOR, 3 WAY
ABC-O-C2   HM   HERMAN MILLER   131.00

** Description: CONNETOR, 2 WAY 90 CORNER
ABC-O-C1   HM   HERMAN MILLER   80.00

** Description: FINISHED END
ABC-O-C3   HM   HERMAN MILLER   19.00

** Description: FLOOR ENTRY, DIRECT CONNECT L
ABC-O-FE   HM   HERMAN MILLER   90.00

** Description: LIGHT, PRIMARY TASK
ABC-O-LT1   HM   HERMAN MILLER   187.00

** Description: PEDESTAL, 2 BOX/1 FILE
ABC-O-PED   HM   HERMAN MILLER   491.00

** Description: POWER JUMPER
ABC-O-PJ   HM   HERMAN MILLER   34.00

** Description: RECEPTACLE CIRCUIT A
ABC-O-DPLX 1   HM   HERMAN MILLER   121.00

** Description: SHELF, OPEN
ABC-O-SH   HM   HERMAN MILLER   175.00

** Description: SINGLE SIDED HARNESS, BELTLINE
ABC-O-EH   HM   HERMAN MILLER   42.00

** Description: STORAGE CABINET
ABC-O-SC   HM   HERMAN MILLER   414.00

** Description: TILE, ACOUSTICAL
ABC-O-T4   HM   HERMAN MILLER   52.00
ABC-O-T5   HM   HERMAN MILLER   61.00
ABC-O-T6   HM   HERMAN MILLER   82.00

7. EXAMPLES

The examples included in this section represent a wide variety of project examples provided by CAD users and publishers. They are oriented primarily toward the architectural user, though several examples are included to show diversity. There is really very little difference between drawings done on AutoCAD and those done on VersaCAD. I hope the inclusion of examples will serve to inspire the user and validate the use of microcomputer aided design in the real world.

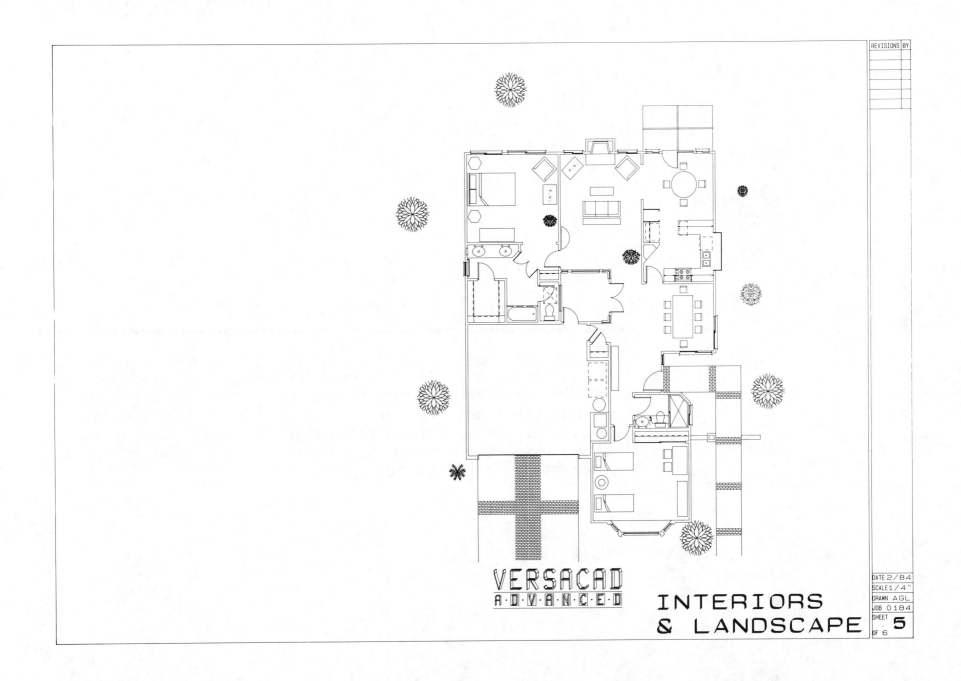

VERSACAD
A·D·V·A·N·C·E·D

INTERIORS
& LANDSCAPE

REVISIONS | BY

DATE 2/84
SCALE 1/4"
DRAWN AGL
JOB 0184
SHEET 5
OF 6

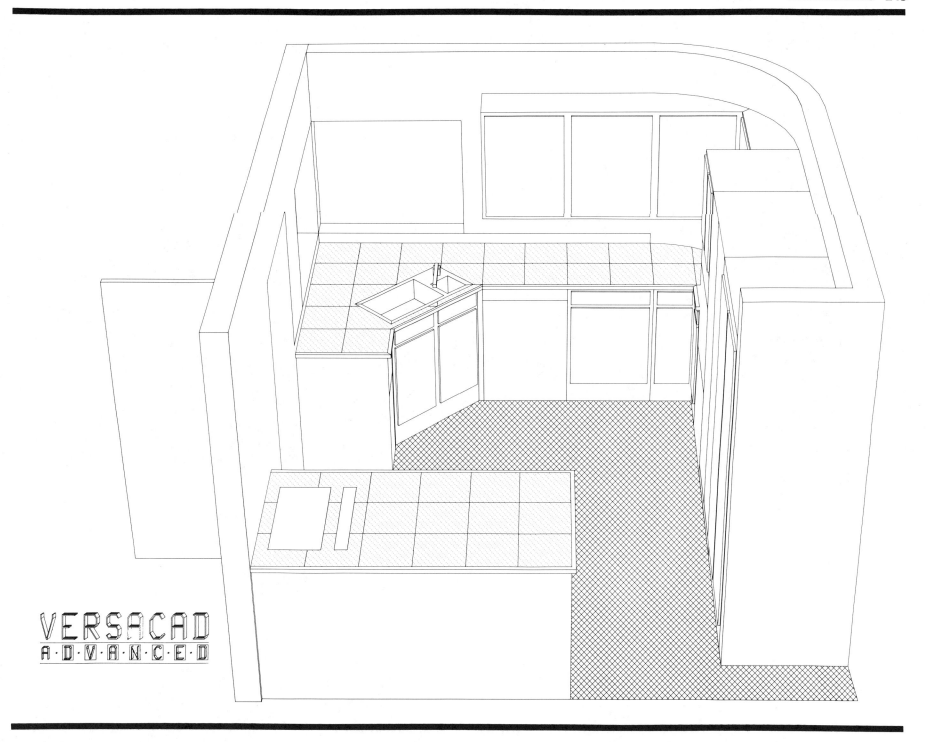

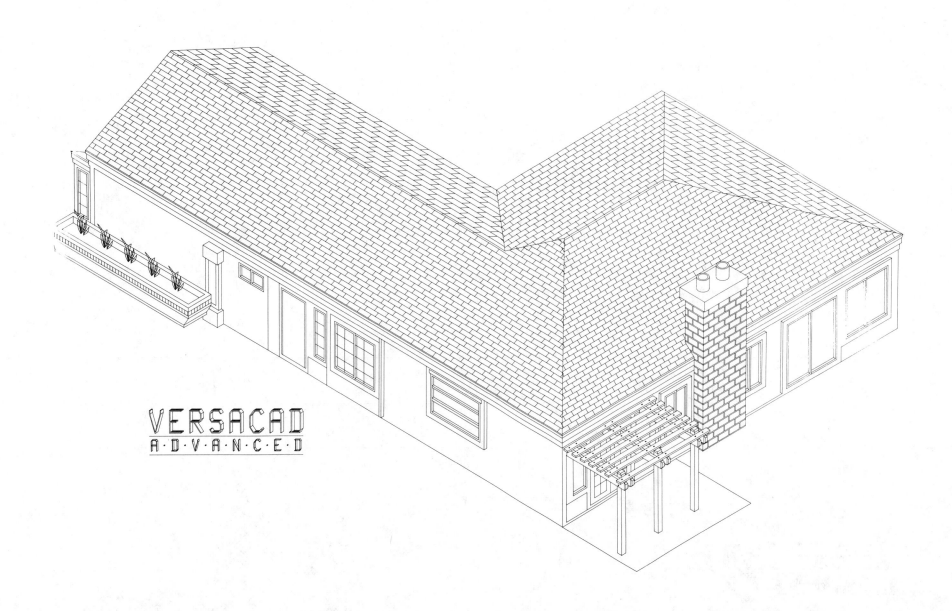

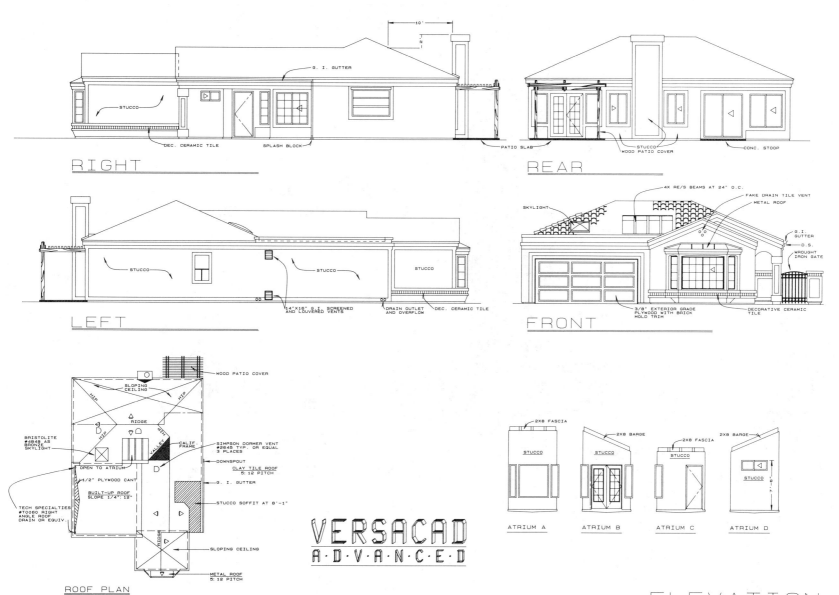

RIGHT

REAR

LEFT

FRONT

ROOF PLAN
SCALE: 1/8"=1'

VERSACAD
A·D·V·A·N·C·E·D

ATRIUM A   ATRIUM B   ATRIUM C   ATRIUM D

2/84
1/4"
AGL
0184

ELEVATION 4

6

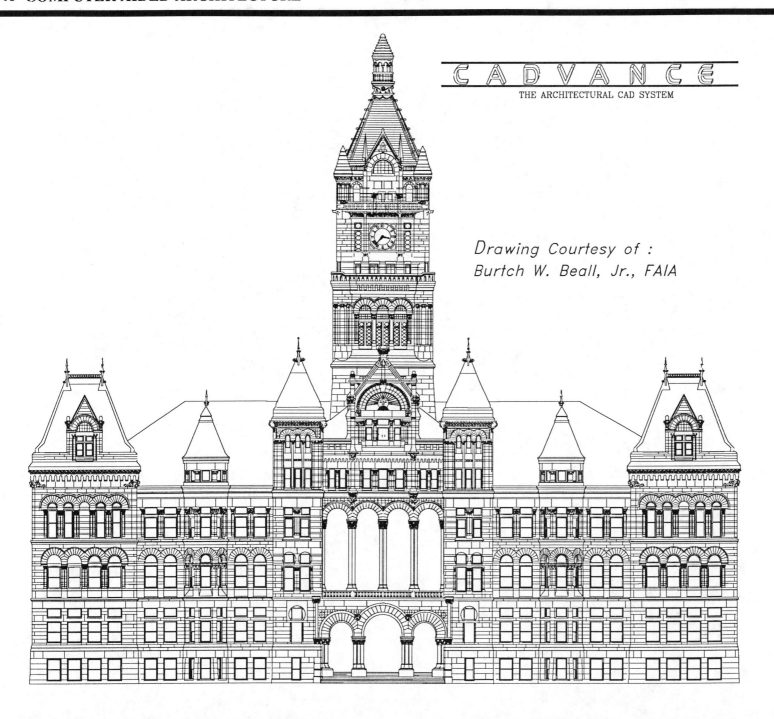

CADVANCE

THE ARCHITECTURAL CAD SYSTEM

Drawing Courtesy of :
Burtch W. Beall, Jr., FAIA

ARCHITECTURAL DETAILS

OFFICE WALL DET ③

LAUNDRY ROOF DET ④⑤

LAUNDRY CRNR DET ⑥

TYP INT LAUNDRY INSUL ⑦
WINDOW CASING & COUNTER
SPLASH SIMILAR

JAMB ⑧ NOTE: LOCATE JAMB IN OPEN'G
FOR BEST POSITION OF
DOOR SADDLE

HEAD ⑨

LAUNDRY DOOR DETAILS

OFFICE DOOR ⑩

HEAD — JAMB SIM ⑪

SILL ⑫

PATIO REPLACEMENT DOORS DETS

DETAIL ⑬
NO SCALE

ISOLATION VALVE DETAIL

NOTE:
DO NOT MANIFOLD
EXHAUST/AIR PIPING
AT MULTIPLE BOILERS

⑭

BOILER BASE DETAIL
NO SCALE

BOILER PIPING AND CONTROL
NO SCALE

OFFICE GATE JAMB ELEVATION

SOLAR WATER HEATING DIAGRAM

CADVANCE
THE ARCHITECTURAL CAD SYSTEM

DRAWING COURTESY OF:
HARALD E. GERBER, A.I.A.

PLOTTED ON:
QMS PostScript Printer

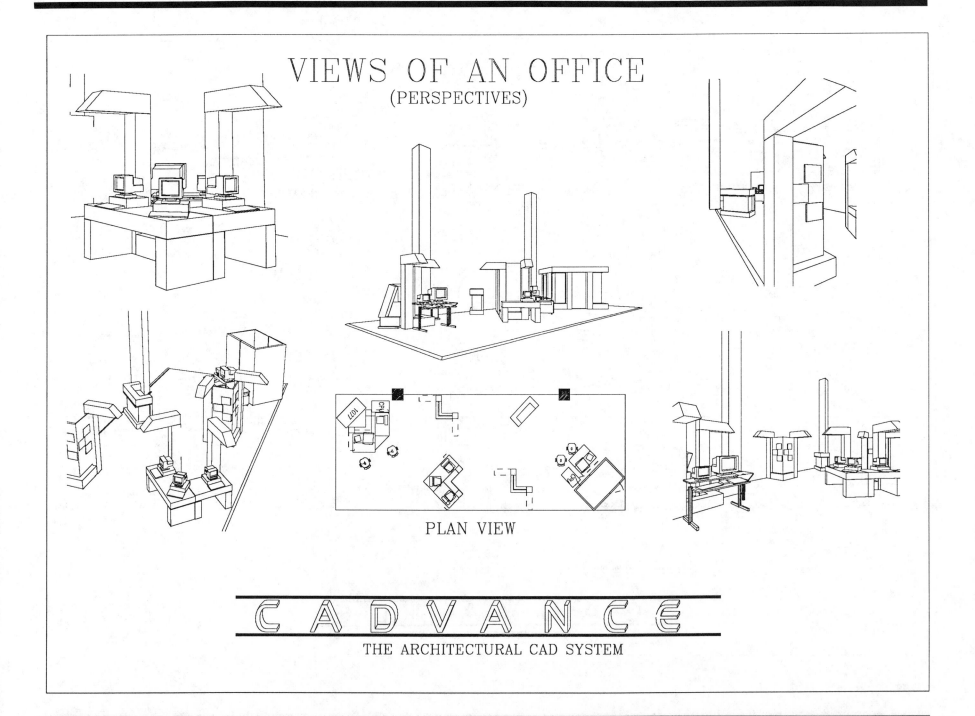

VIEWS OF AN OFFICE

(PERSPECTIVES)

PLAN VIEW

CADVANCE

THE ARCHITECTURAL CAD SYSTEM

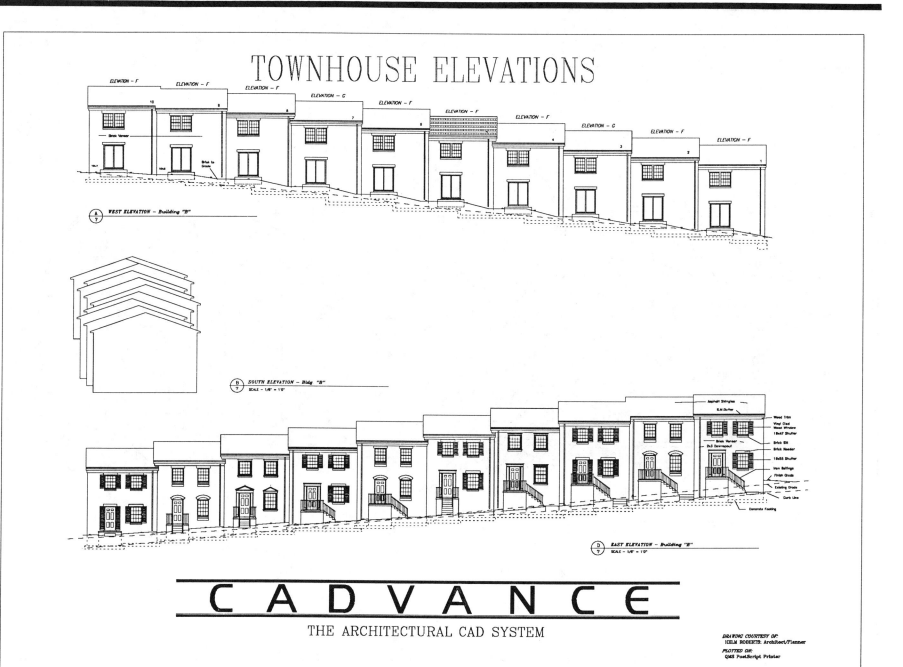

TOWNHOUSE ELEVATIONS

WEST ELEVATION – Building "B"

SOUTH ELEVATION – Bldg "B"
SCALE – 1/8" = 1'0"

EAST ELEVATION – Building "B"
SCALE – 1/8" = 1'0"

C A D V A N C E

THE ARCHITECTURAL CAD SYSTEM

DRAWING COURTESY OF:
HELM ROBERTS: Architect/Planner
PLOTTED ON:
QMS PostScript Printer

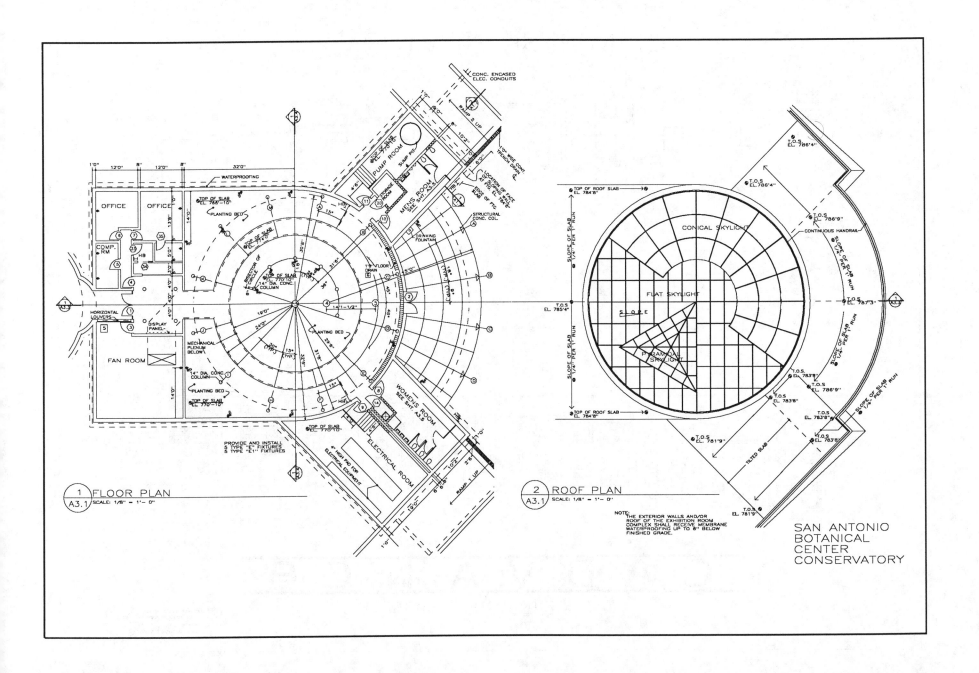

1 FLOOR PLAN
A3.1 SCALE: 1/8" = 1'-0"

2 ROOF PLAN
A3.1 SCALE: 1/8" = 1'-0"

NOTE:
THE EXTERIOR WALLS AND/OR
ROOF OF THE EXHIBITION ROOM
COMPLEX SHALL RECEIVE MEMBRANE
WATERPROOFING UP TO 8" BELOW
FINISHED GRADE.

SAN ANTONIO
BOTANICAL
CENTER
CONSERVATORY

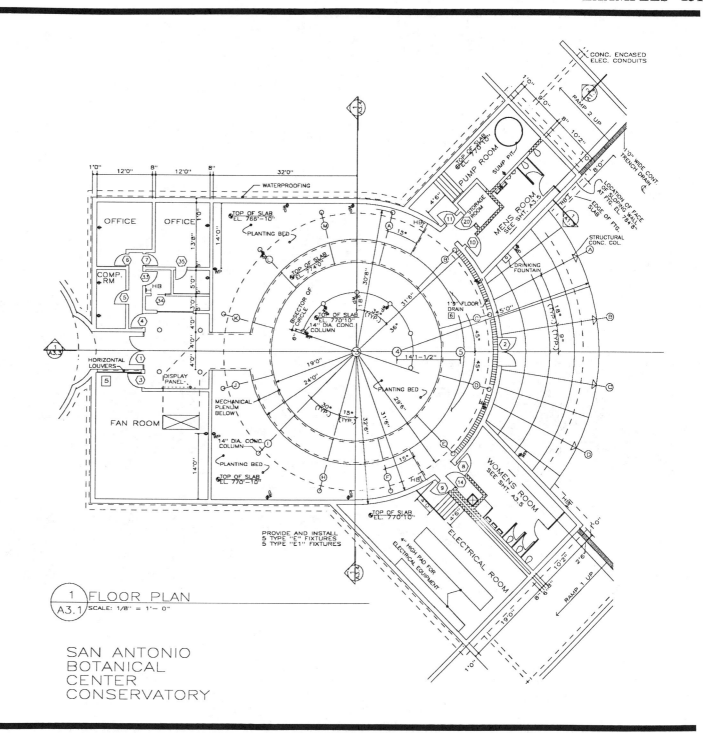

1 FLOOR PLAN
A3.1 SCALE: 1/8" = 1'- 0"

SAN ANTONIO
BOTANICAL
CENTER
CONSERVATORY

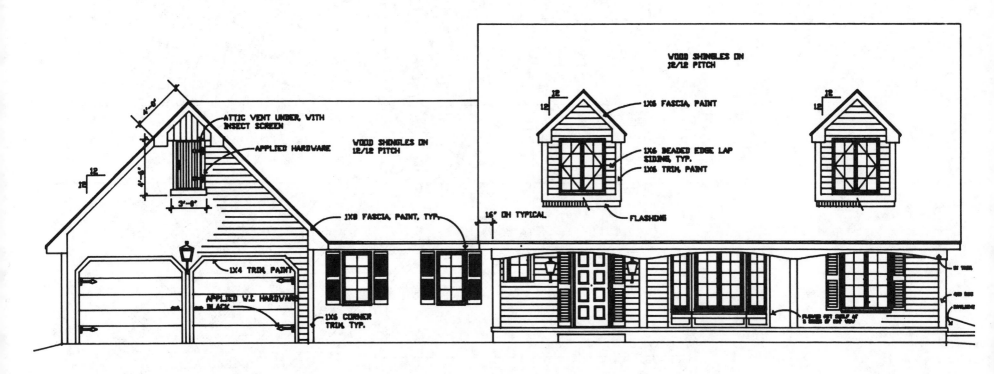

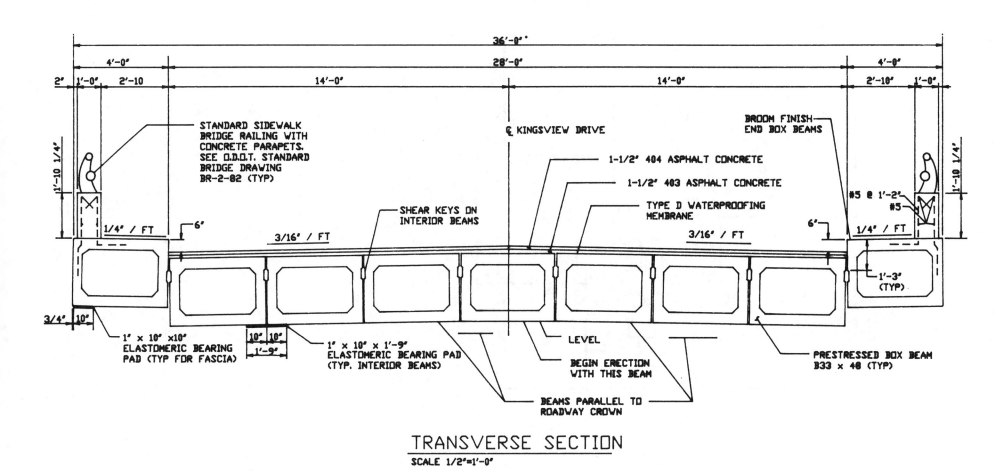

STANDARD SIDEWALK
BRIDGE RAILING WITH
CONCRETE PARAPETS.
SEE O.D.O.T. STANDARD
BRIDGE DRAWING
BR-2-82 (TYP)

BROOM FINISH
END BOX BEAMS

₵ KINGSVIEW DRIVE

1-1/2" 404 ASPHALT CONCRETE

1-1/2" 403 ASPHALT CONCRETE

TYPE D WATERPROOFING
MEMBRANE

SHEAR KEYS ON
INTERIOR BEAMS

#5 @ 1'-2"
#5

36'-0"

4'-0"

28'-0"

4'-0"

2" 1'-0" 2'-10"

14'-0"

14'-0"

2'-10" 1'-0"

1'-10 1/4"

1'-10 1/4"

1/4" / FT

6"

3/16" / FT

3/16" / FT

6"

1/4" / FT

1'-3"
(TYP)

3/4" 10"

1' × 10" ×10"
ELASTOMERIC BEARING
PAD (TYP FOR FASCIA)

10" 10"
1'-9"

1' × 10" × 1'-9"
ELASTOMERIC BEARING PAD
(TYP. INTERIOR BEAMS)

LEVEL

BEGIN ERECTION
WITH THIS BEAM

PRESTRESSED BOX BEAM
B33 × 48 (TYP)

BEAMS PARALLEL TO
ROADWAY CROWN

TRANSVERSE SECTION
SCALE 1/2"=1'-0"

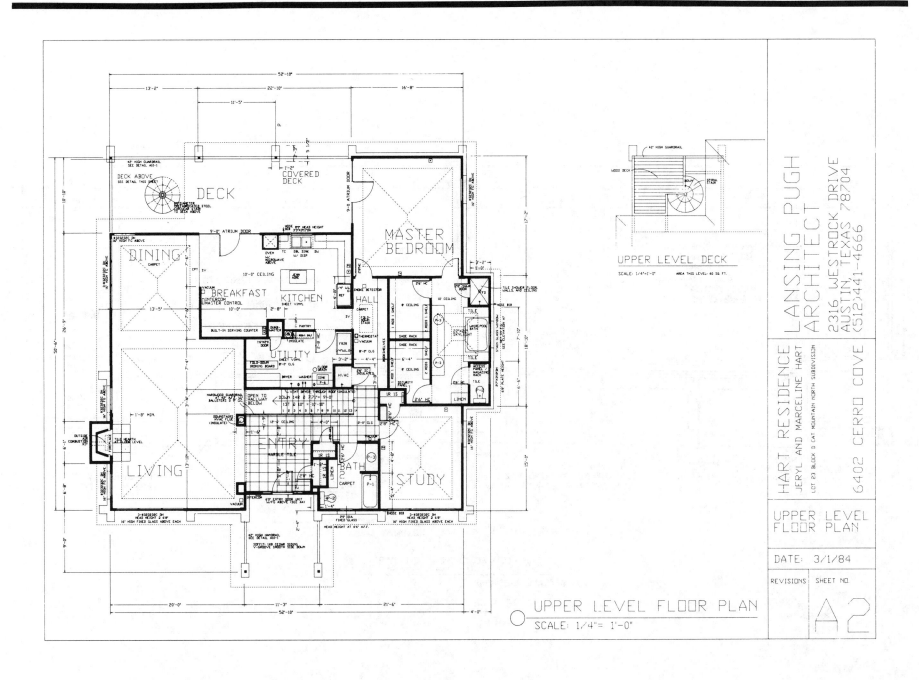

UPPER LEVEL DECK

SCALE: 1/4"=1'-0"   AREA THIS LEVEL: 60 SQ. FT.

UPPER LEVEL FLOOR PLAN

SCALE: 1/4"= 1'-0"

HART RESIDENCE
JERYL AND MARCELINE HART
LOT 23 BLOCK D CAT MOUNTAIN NORTH SUBDIVISION

LANSING PUGH
ARCHITECT
2316 WESTROCK DRIVE
AUSTIN, TEXAS 78704
(512) 441-4666

6402 CERRO COVE

UPPER LEVEL
FLOOR PLAN

DATE: 3/1/84

REVISIONS   SHEET NO.

A2

6 X 12 RSC TIMBERS
TYP ABOVE VDVS

2X RSC SHUTTERS

FULL BRICK

BRICK CORBEL
BRACKET

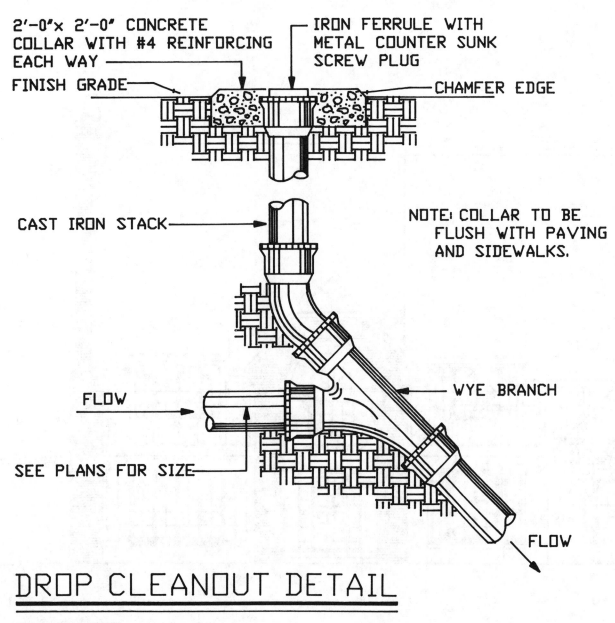

2'-0"x 2'-0" CONCRETE
COLLAR WITH #4 REINFORCING
EACH WAY

IRON FERRULE WITH
METAL COUNTER SUNK
SCREW PLUG

FINISH GRADE

CHAMFER EDGE

CAST IRON STACK

NOTE: COLLAR TO BE
FLUSH WITH PAVING
AND SIDEWALKS.

FLOW

WYE BRANCH

SEE PLANS FOR SIZE

FLOW

DROP CLEANOUT DETAIL

SCALE: NONE

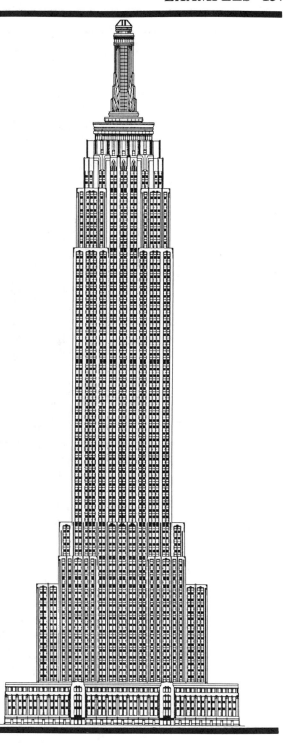

TURBO DESIGNER

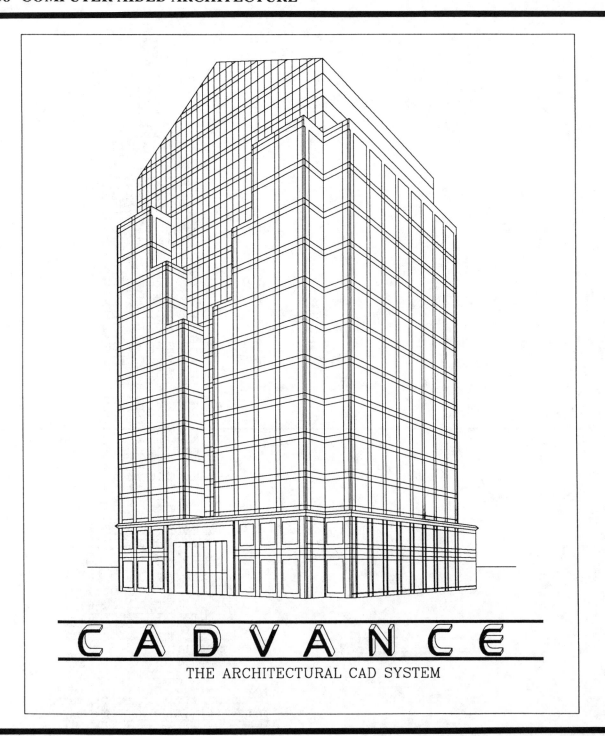

THE ARCHITECTURAL CAD SYSTEM

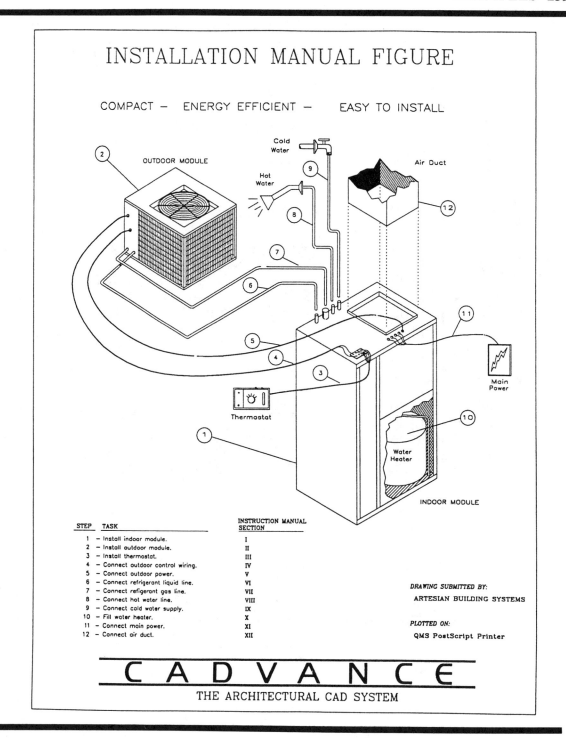

INSTALLATION MANUAL FIGURE

COMPACT — ENERGY EFFICIENT — EASY TO INSTALL

STEP	TASK	INSTRUCTION MANUAL SECTION
1	— Install indoor module.	I
2	— Install outdoor module.	II
3	— Install thermostat.	III
4	— Connect outdoor control wiring.	IV
5	— Connect outdoor power.	V
6	— Connect refrigerant liquid line.	VI
7	— Connect refrigerant gas line.	VII
8	— Connect hot water line.	VIII
9	— Connect cold water supply.	IX
10	— Fill water heater.	X
11	— Connect main power.	XI
12	— Connect air duct.	XII

DRAWING SUBMITTED BY:

ARTESIAN BUILDING SYSTEMS

PLOTTED ON:

QMS PostScript Printer

CADVANCE
THE ARCHITECTURAL CAD SYSTEM

PERSPECTIVE PROJECTIONS

 0 ft station height

 5 ft

 10 ft

 16 ft

 −16 ft starting height
8 ft high walls (typ)

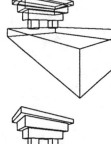

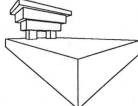

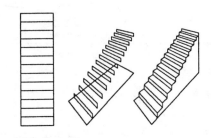

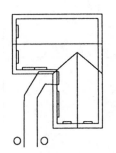

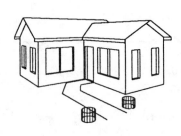

CADVANCE

THE ARCHITECTURAL CAD SYSTEM

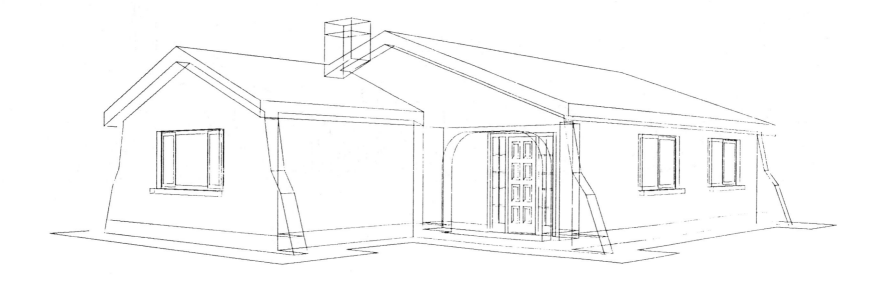

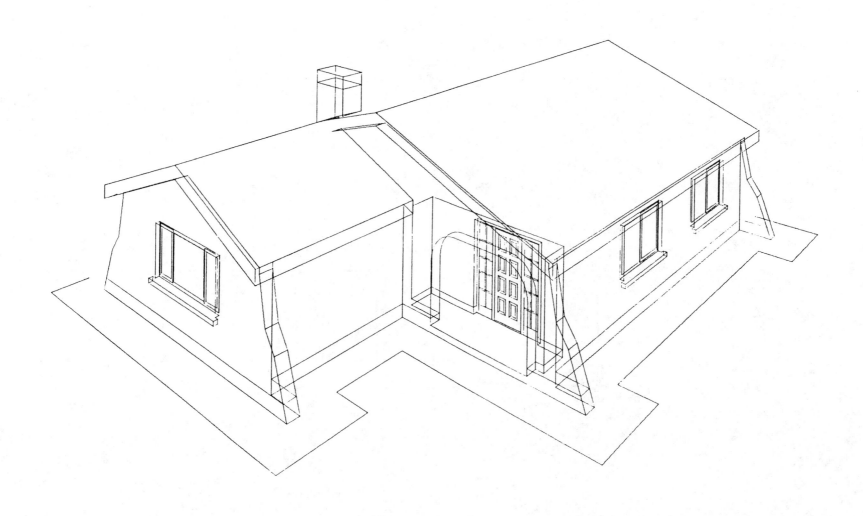

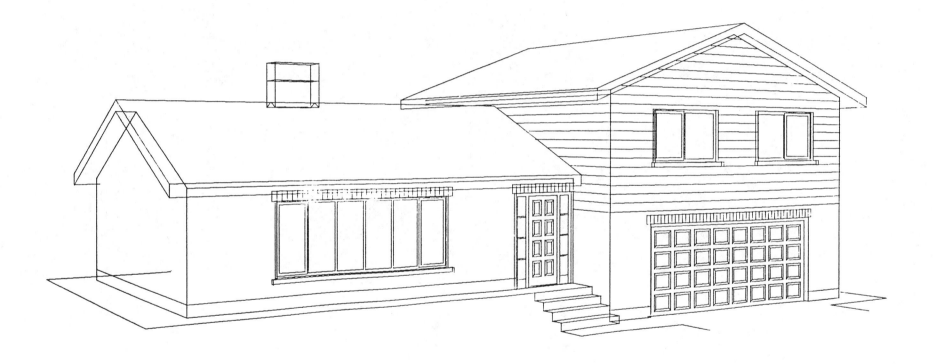

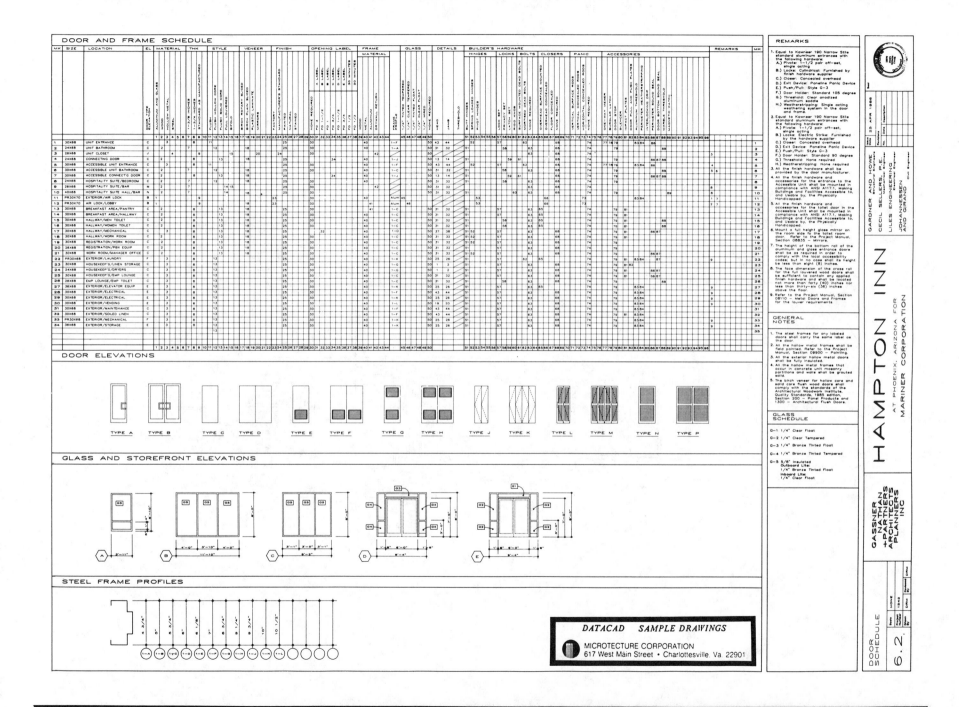

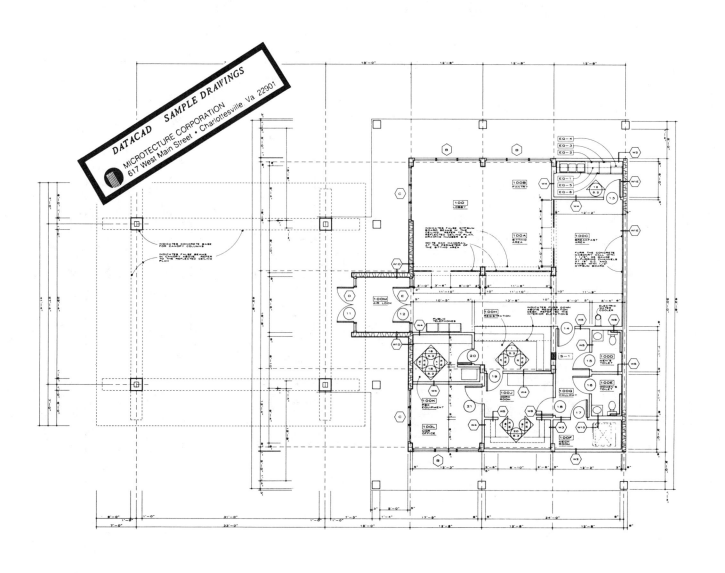

EQUIPMENT SCHEDULE

EQ-1   Three (3) Compartment
       Stainless Steel Sink
EQ-2   Undercounter Dishwasher
EQ-3   Undercounter Refrigerator
EQ-4   Undercounter Ice Maker
EQ-5   Wall Cabinets
EQ-6   Base Cabinets

SPECIALTY SCHEDULE

S-1   Recessed Fire Extinguisher Cabinet
      with a Ten (10) Pound ABC Multi-
      Purpose Portable Fire Extinguisher

GENERAL NOTES

1. Refer to the Project Manual for the amount of the allowance under which the Decorative Quarry Tile is to be purchased.

2. All carpet, related pad and installation shall be provided by the Owner.

3. All the carpet accessories, such as the rubber or vinyl edge strips, saddles and reducers, where the carpet abuts vinyl or rubber flooring, will be provided by the Owner.

4. All the manmade marble thresholds where the carpet abuts ceramic or other hard tile shall be provided by the Contractor.

5. All the casework, cabinets and countertops in Registration 100H shall be provided by the Contractor.

6. All the casework, cabinets and countertops in Work Room 100J shall be provided by the Contractor.

7. All the casework, countertops and shelving in PBX 100K shall be provided by the Contractor. The Contractor shall ascertain the weights of the equipment to be supported by the shelving and shall adequately brace and reinforce the supporting partitions.

8. All the casework, cabinets and countertops in Pantry 100B shall be provided by the Contractor.

9. The following items of equipment shall be furnished by the Owner and installed by the Contractor: EQ-2, EQ-3, and EQ-4. The stainless steel sink (EQ-1) shall be provided by the Contractor.

HAMPTON INN

AT PHOENIX, ARIZONA FOR
MARINER CORPORATION

GARDNER AND HOWE
Structural Engineers
CECIL SELLERS, P.E.

LILES ENGINEERING
Electrical Engineer

JOHANNESSEN
AND GIRAND
Civil Engineer

GASSNER
+PARTNERS
ARCHITECTS
PLANNERS
INC

LOBBY FLOOR PLAN

5.1

NORTH

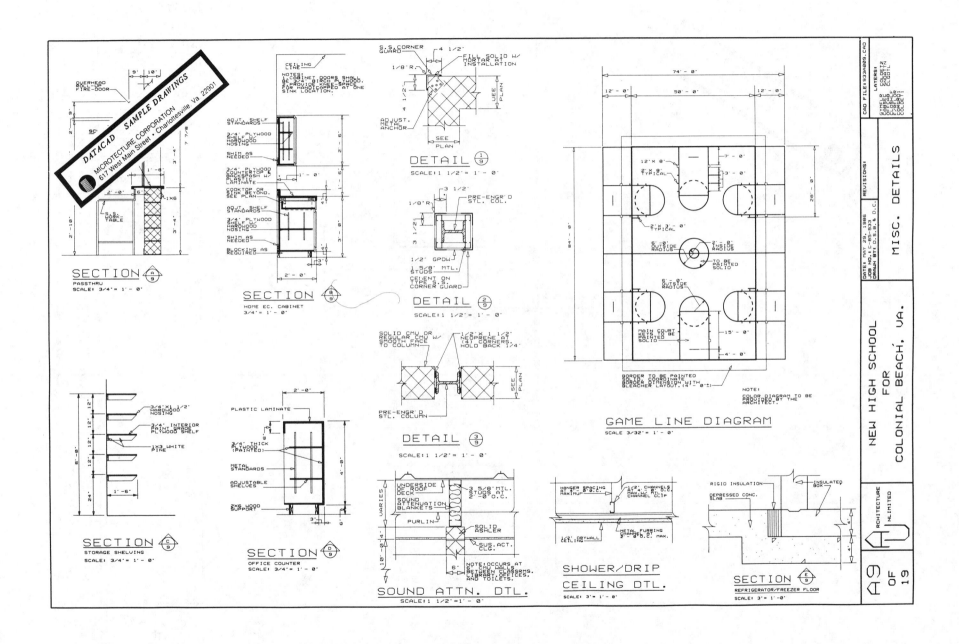

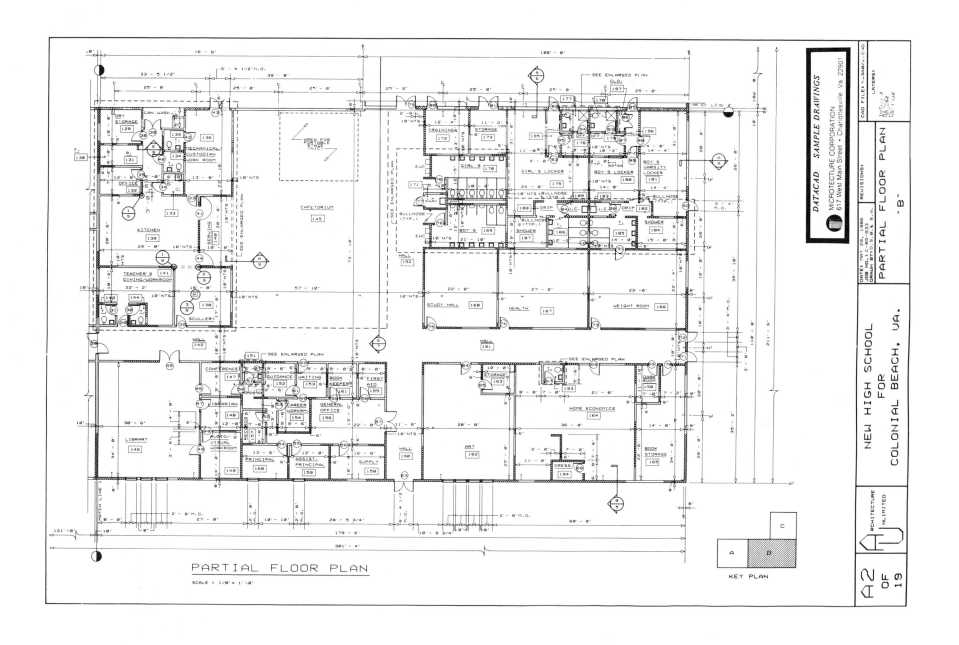

PARTIAL FLOOR PLAN

SCALE : 1/8" = 1'-0"

KEY PLAN

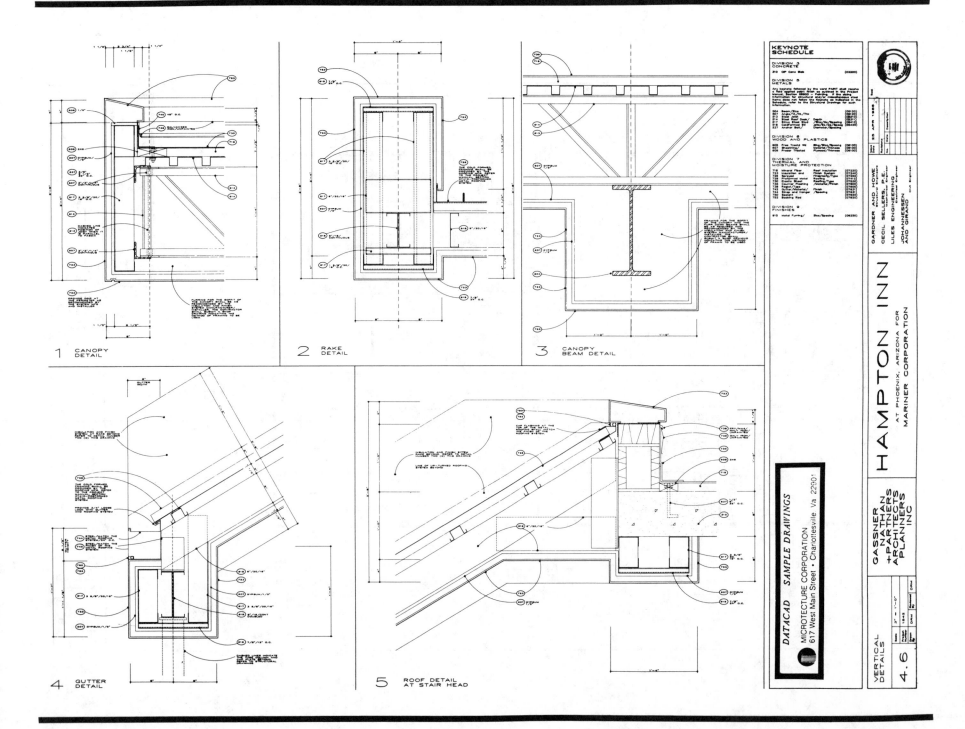

1 CANOPY DETAIL

2 RAKE DETAIL

3 CANOPY BEAM DETAIL

4 GUTTER DETAIL

5 ROOF DETAIL AT STAIR HEAD

DATACAD SAMPLE DRAWINGS

MICROTECTURE CORPORATION
617 West Main Street • Charlottesville Va 22901

GASSNER
NATHAN
+PARTNERS
ARCHITECTS
PLANNERS
INC

HAMPTON INN
AT PHOENIX, ARIZONA FOR
MARINER CORPORATION

GARDNER AND HOWE
Structural Engineers
CECIL SELLERS, P.E.
LILES ENGINEERING
Mechanical Engineer
JOHANNESSEN
AND GIRAND
Civil Engineer

VERTICAL DETAILS

4.6

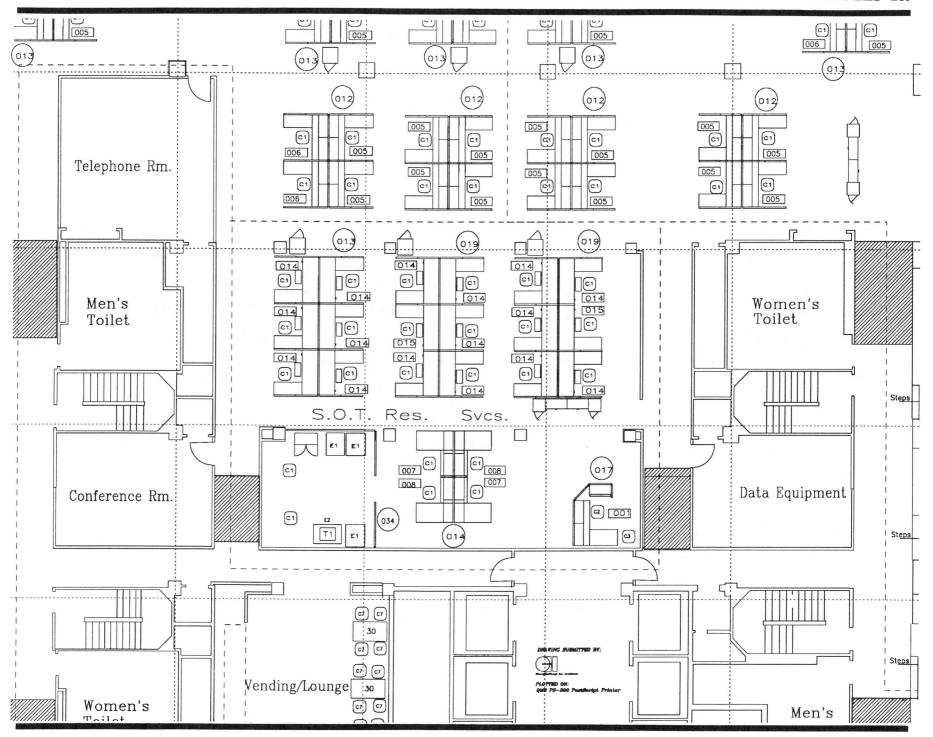

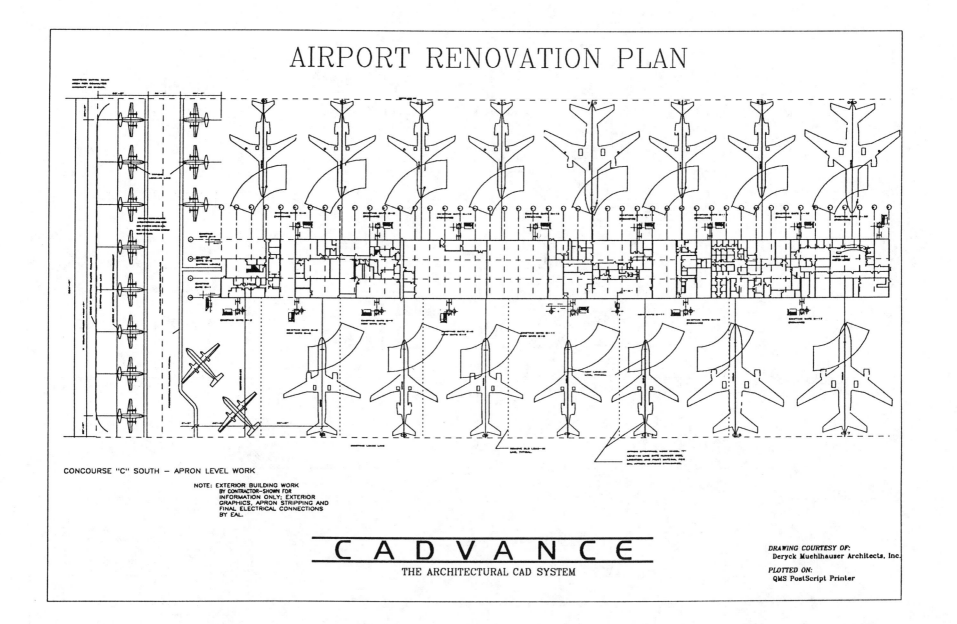

AIRPORT RENOVATION PLAN

CONCOURSE "C" SOUTH – APRON LEVEL WORK

NOTE: EXTERIOR BUILDING WORK
BY CONTRACTOR–SHOWN FOR
INFORMATION ONLY; EXTERIOR
GRAPHICS, APRON STRIPPING AND
FINAL ELECTRICAL CONNECTIONS
BY EAL.

CADVANCE
THE ARCHITECTURAL CAD SYSTEM

DRAWING COURTESY OF:
Deryck Muehlhauser Architects, Inc.

PLOTTED ON:
QMS PostScript Printer

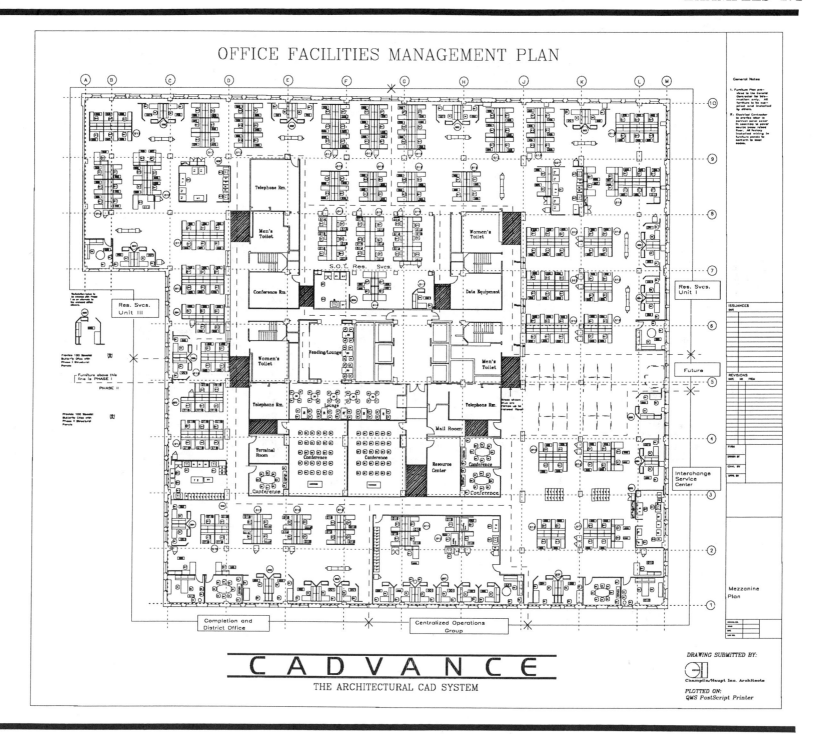

OFFICE FACILITIES MANAGEMENT PLAN

CADVANCE
THE ARCHITECTURAL CAD SYSTEM

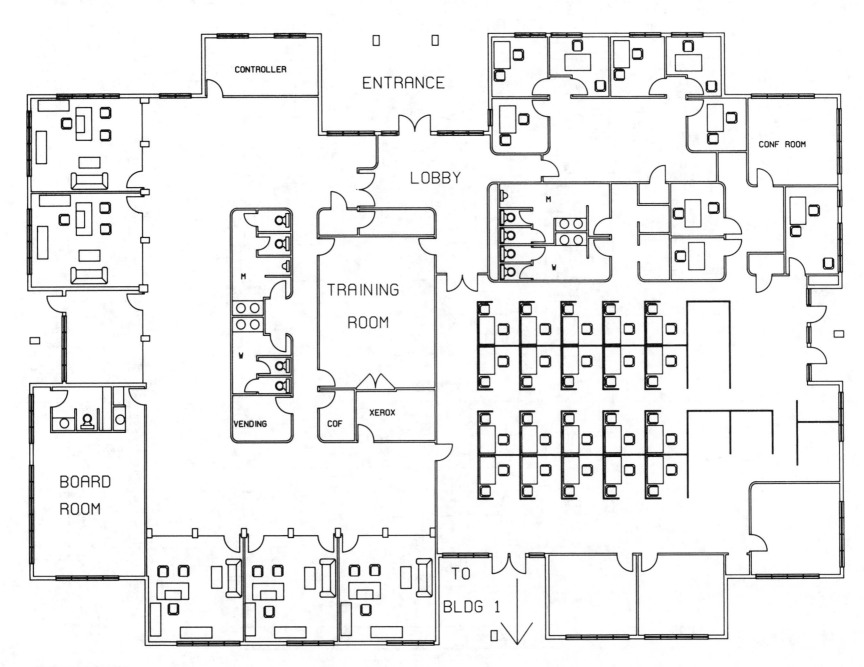

CONTROLLER

ENTRANCE

CONF ROOM

LOBBY

M

W

TRAINING

ROOM

M

W

VENDING

COF

XEROX

BOARD

ROOM

TO

BLDG 1

Plots supplied by CalComp PSU

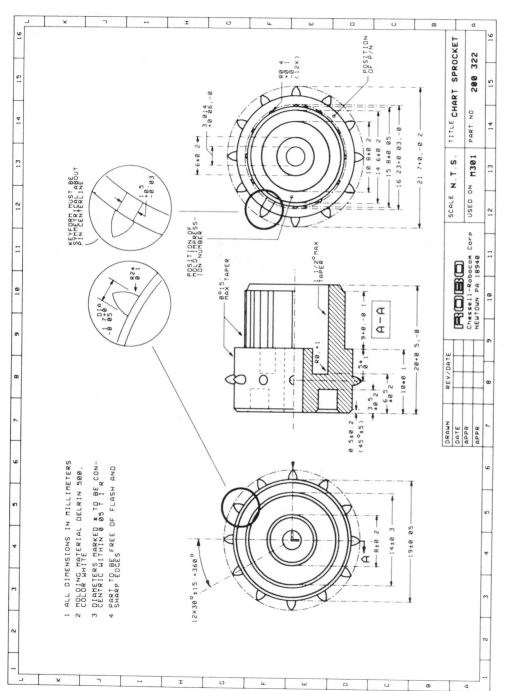

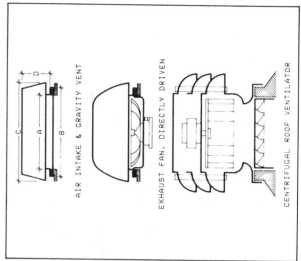

AIR INTAKE & GRAVITY VENT

EXHAUST FAN, DIRECTLY DRIVEN

CENTRIFUGAL ROOF VENTILATOR

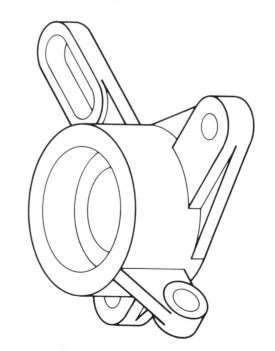

Photo-reductions of drawings plotted with RoboCAD systems for Apple II and *IIe*.

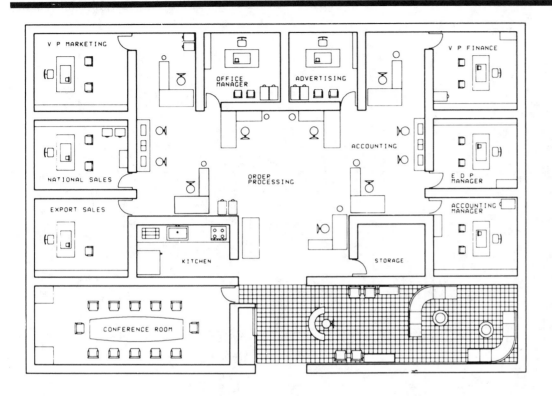

ROBO SYSTEMS

ROBO SYSTEMS CORPORATION
Newtown, PA 18940 (215) 968-4422

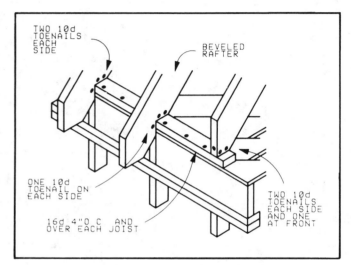

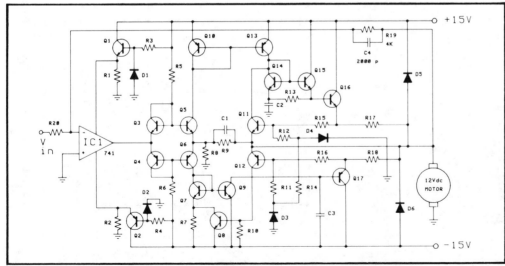

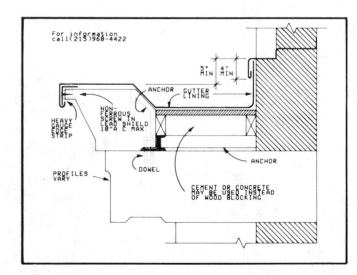

Photo-reductions of drawings plotted with RoboCAD systems for Apple II and IIe.

Designed by MicroCAD^{tm}

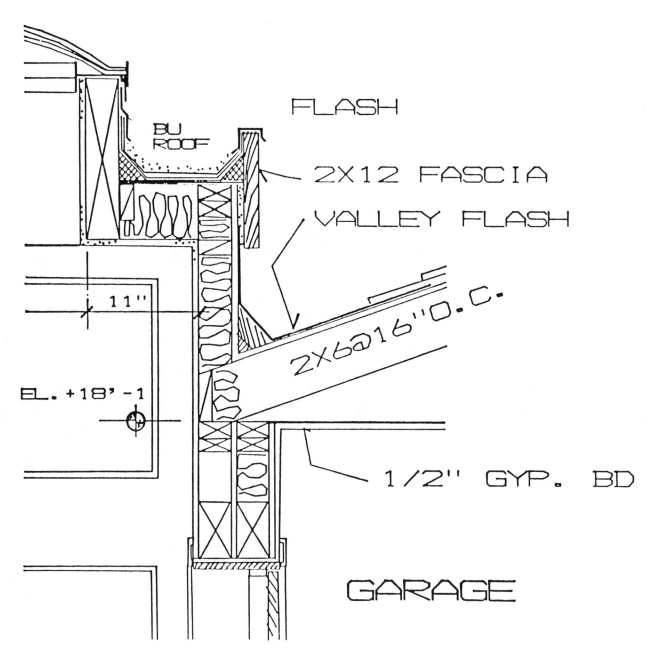

FLASH

2X12 FASCIA

VALLEY FLASH

BU ROOF

2X6@16"O.C.

11"

EL. +18'-1

1/2" GYP. BD

GARAGE

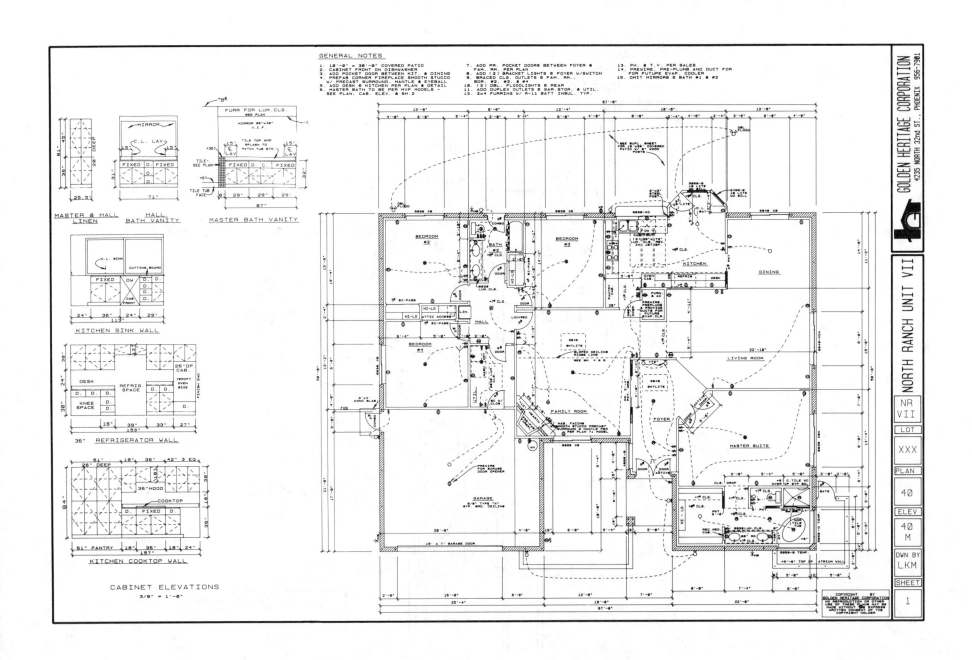

CABINET ELEVATIONS
3/8" = 1'-0"

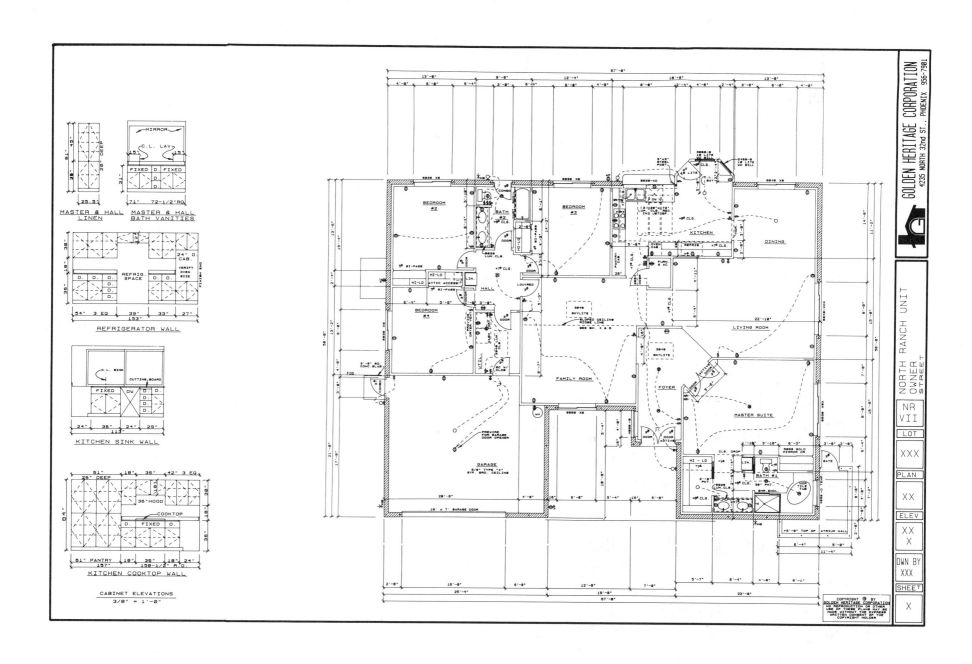

MASTER & HALL
LINEN

MASTER & HALL
BATH VANITIES

REFRIGERATOR WALL

KITCHEN SINK WALL

KITCHEN COOKTOP WALL

CABINET ELEVATIONS
3/8" = 1'-0"

GOLDEN HERITAGE CORPORATION
4235 NORTH 32nd ST., PHOENIX 956-7901

NORTH RANCH UNIT
OWNER
STREET

NR
VII

LOT
XXX

PLAN
XX

ELEV
XX
X

DWN BY
XXX

SHEET
X

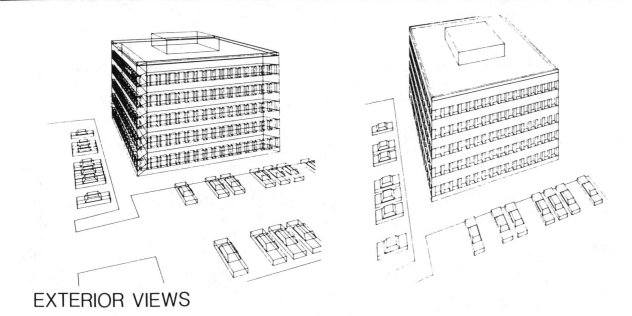

EXTERIOR VIEWS

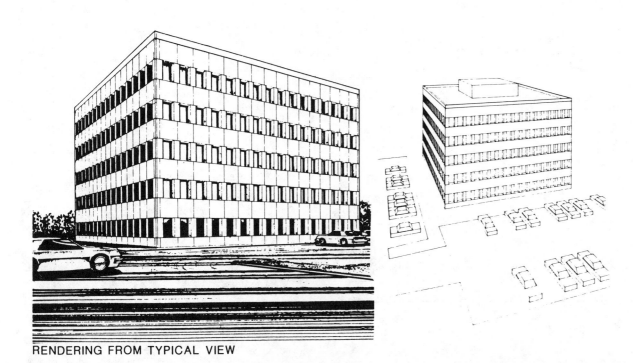

RENDERING FROM TYPICAL VIEW

APPENDIX A

HARDWARE

The hardware chapter intends to give a basic overview of the hardware required for the microcomputer CAD system. I make no attempt to be comprehensive but rather to give a simple introduction. The user is well served to work in the acquisition of computers and other hardware with an established dealer who can provide installation, training and service. Mail order savings are best reserved for individuals who are well versed in the complex computer systems. Any savings the neophyte might initially gain can quickly be lost in service calls.

COMPUTER

The computer itself is the most important element in the CAD system. It is the center of operations. There are a wide variety of computers available in the microcomputer world to operate CAD. The best established and the first serious professional software systems in this class were written for and sold on the IBM PC. This system, in its original form, as well as its derivations, still dominates the market. This market dominance, however, is due to change soon with the advent of more sophisiticated graphics units and increasing demand for high speed and higher resolution displays.

The most widely used current version of the IBM PC is the PC AT and its compatibles, such as the AT&T 6300 Plus. These machines with their Intel 80286 processing chips are significantly faster and more sophisticated than the earlier IBM PC class machines. There are few serious users who choose anything less than these computers, except for entry level and training purposes, due to their significantly better performance and modest price differential.

While the PC AT class machine is currently dominant, the IBM RT and dedicated graphics workstations from such sources as SUN and APOLLO are challenging the price performance ratio of the general purpose AT's. I believe that, at the writing of this book, the future of computer graphics capability and price is due for significant change to the advantage of the serious CAD user.

In selecting a computer for your use remember to consider speed and compatibility with your software and hardware needs, within the demands you will place on the hardware in your work environment. There is no universally ideal machine, only the relatively ideal one. In using CAD, you must also remember that the peripherals and graphics display devices are as important as the computer itself.

COPROCESSORS

A coprocessor is a computer chip that aids the primary central processing unit in making the calculations necessary to process the information at hand. The cental processing chips used in IBM PC's, such as the Intel 8088 and 80286, can not do multiplication and division directly. Those processes have to be done within the software. This slows the process of calculating vectors in a CAD drawing dramatically. The math coprocessor chips such as the 8087 and 80287 take over this process within the hardware, and can speed the computations by many times.

Any serious CAD application which depends on floating point calculation within their database structure can benefit greatly from the installation of a math coprocessor in the socket provided by the computer manufacturer. Most CAD software systems use the floating point system (as opposed to the integer method). The cost of this additional chip is nominal compared to improved performance.

DIGITIZERS

A magnetic tablet with a stylus pointer or puck with cross hairs is used to input coordinate information into digital form for processing by a computer. In CAD it is the device and process of indirectly or directly reading drawing information into the machine. A digitizer also serves as a cursor pointing device, as does a mouse, however it is much more accurate (up to .001").

In architectural work, the value of digitizing a drawing is questionable. In most cases it is faster and more accurate to redraw the plans directly into the system. A digitizer comes into its strong point when used with predetermined templates of commands and symbols, such as the Turbo Designer template described Chapter 4. Some CAD systems support the strengths of a digitizer more than others. Before spending the extra money for a digitizer, make sure that your system and needs demand one.

DISPLAY CARDS

The display card and its related monitor are probably the next most important elements in hardware selection. The importance of accuracy and ease of drawing, dependent on the resolution and type of CRT display used in the system, can't be overemphasized. The user should select the highest resolution color system he or she can afford.

In the earliest days of the IBM PC world, there was a choice between the low resolution (320 x 200 pixels) of the Color Graphics Adapter, and the third party monochrome graphic board make by Hercules (720 x 360 pixels). The current choices have a much wider range, up to 2000+ pixel resolution, at a variety of prices. The current acceptable resolution range for professional CAD starts with the IBM EGA, or enhanced graphics adapter, with a resolution of 640 x 350 pixels in color. There are a number of EGA clones available. A higher resolution device is desirable, but price versus performance should be considered. Any display device chosen should be "non-interlaced," or write directly all the horizontal lines from memory. Interlaced schemes tend to flicker and cause operator fatigue.

MICE

A mouse is a hand-held cursor control/input device attached to the computer. There are a number of mouse types including mechanical, optical and opto-mechanical, with one, two or three buttons. The best for you is determined by personal preference. The mouse is the least expensive professional input device and will work with most, if not all systems. The mouse is not accurate enough to use in digitizing a drawing, but is more than adequate for all other purposes. They are handy to use with software other than the CAD system.

MONITORS

The cathode ray tube used to display graphic and other information from the computer is called a monitor, CRT or display. This is used in concert with the display adapter to display the information from your computer. The quality and resolution of the monitor should be coordinated with the display adapter. The lower resolution displays are digital, while the higher ones are analog and digital. The scan rate is expressed in Megahertz or Mhz. Typically, the higher the Mhz rating, the higher the resolution. The scan rate must be matched with the display adapter. If they are not coordinated, system failure or damage may occur.

PLOTTERS

The hardcopy graphic output device used to prepare a drawing is called a plotter. The method used varies from computer-controlled moving pens to eletrostatic processes similar to photocopy machines. The moving pen variety are the most inexpensive, while the electrostatic are the most expensive. Prices range from several hundred dollars for 8-1/2" x 11" pen plotters to $100,000+ for large and fast electrostatic machines.

The typical architectural office can suffice with a modest pen plotter which handles the sheet sizes required for their office. The typical professional grade D or E sized plotter will cost $5000 to $10,000. The D size plotter is generally the architectural requirement. A less expensive A and B size plotter can serve as a second unit at a much reduced price or a multi-sheet-size plotter can be purchased.

SOFTWARE

This chapter presents some of the major publishers of microcomputer CAD software serving the architectural community at publication time. It is not exhaustive either in its listings or in its treatment of the products the respective companies offer. The industry and its products are changing much too fast for a compendium to be more than passingly useful as a detailed evaluation or index of available products.

What I intend here is a brief overview of the current microcomputer CAD products, with some small confidence that they will maintain that general direction in the future. I will also mention current and announced products with the clear understanding of my readers that this is not definitive data.

Another basic assumption is that, with relatively minor exception, most of the basic functions of a professional CAD system, such as automatic dimensioning, levels or layering, are supported by all the systems listed.

AT&T Corporation
1000 Pittsford-Victor Road
Pittsford, N.Y. 14534

716-385-8500

Primary Product:

AT&T sells a version of the VersaCAD system which is generally bundled with the AT&T personal computer. There is little if any difference in the **OmniDraft** system and VersaCAD.

Other Products:

Libraries and templates as well as hardware.

Autodesk, Inc.
2320 Marinship Way
Sausalito, Ca 94965

415-332-2344

Primary Product:

AutoCAD is the largest selling microcomputer CAD software package. This system is noted for its programability and extensive third-party software support. The system is available on most PC computers as well as many engineering graphics workstations. Though this system is a general purpose system, enhancements from third-party developers like Creative Technologies with its Turbo Designer make the system an important one for the architectural user to consider.

Other Products:

CAD/camera, software for automatic digitizing of existing paper drawings. **AE/CADD**, an architectural overlay template to customize AutoCAD for the architectural user.

CADAM INC.
1935 North Buena Vista Street
Burbank, Ca 91504

818-841-9470

Primary Product:

Cadam Inc. is a subsidiary of Lockheed Corporation and is the developer and publisher of CADAM and Professional CADAM, the largest selling large computer CAD systems. The **MICRO CADAM** product is a fully integrated subset of the large systems designed to be free standing workstations which can integrate and share files with its larger siblings. This system is traditionally directed toward mechanical and manufacturing application but the size of its parent market indicates that this system should be of interest to architects and designers in general and those who have Fortune 500 clients with the large CADAM systems.

Other Products:

CADAM and **Professional CADAM.**

Computervision Corp.
2 Crosby Drive
Bedford, Ma 01730

617-275-1800

Primary Product:

For the architect the **Personal Architect** is a design system with aspect of 2D, 3D and data management rolled into one, with elements of design development included. At this writing the system is powerful and holds great promise but needs much more research and development to become a primary design tool in the average office. Computervision makes major large-system CAD products and is a major market leader here.

Other Products:

Mainframe and minicomputer systems, utilities, modules and libraries. Similar products for engineering.

DiGiTAL Matrix Services, Inc.
59 Merrick Way, Suite 201
Coral Gables, Fl. 33134

305-445-1749

Primary Product:

DiGiCAD is a microcomputer system that emulates many of the alphanumeric database functions of mainframe CAD systems. Its alphanumeric database is integrated bi-directionally with the graphic database which allows the user to query the data from either information display. This system was focused initially on civil engineering but has many attributes to offer the architect or designer.

Other Products:

DiGiTAL is currently offering the **DiGiTRAN** applications development package for programmers, business graphics development program and symbol and template libraries for various industries and services.

Imagimedia Technologies Inc.
P.O. Box 210308
San Francisco, Ca 94121-0308

415-387-0263

Primary Products:

MicroCAD was the first CAD system released for the IBM PC and remains one of the most innovative 3D oriented systems for the small computer. The system is a fully integrated 2D and 3D system though the emphasis is on 3D design. MicroCAD allows full perspective drawing and visualization in real time rather than plan and elevation projections or extrusions. The system supports the VDI graphic standard.

Other Products:

Personal Secretary time management system. Various modules and symbol libraries. Can read and write to AutoCAD, VersaCAD and other major 2D systems.

Manufacturing and Consulting Services, Inc.
9500 Toledo Way
Irvine, Ca 92718

800-932-9329

Primary Product:

Anvil 1000MD is the microcomputer-based 3D system which has been ported from this company's large-system CAD. Its greatest user base by far is in the mechanical design world, but it is a powerful 3D package of interest to the architectural user as well.

Other Products:

Mainframe and minicomputer versions and utilities.

Mega Cadd Inc.
401 Second Avenue South
Seattle, Wa 98104

800-223-3175

Primary Product:

Mega Cadd's major product is called **Design Board Professional** however it is more widely known as MegaCADD. This system is an architecturally oriented 3D design system that utilizes a shape and surface method of creating wire frame drawings. It has hidden line removal rotations and projections as would be expected in a professional system. The system can share files with AutoCAD, Cadvance, VersaCAD and other systems.

Other Products:

Design Board Illustrator solid paint program which works with wire-frame images produced by Design Board Professional.

Microtecture Corporation
218 W. Main Street,
Charlottesville, Va 22901

804-295-2600

Primary Product:

DataCAD is advertised as CAD by architects for architects and this is true. This system is oriented in its design and documentation for the architectural user. It has an integrated data system and is integrated with 3D for design as well as drafting. The system is also unique in the microcomputer world in its companion integrated architectural accounting system.

Other Products:

A full architectural accounting package. A three-dimensional design package. Symbol libraries.

Point Line Co.
2280 Powell Street
San Francisco, Ca 94113

415-989-0444

Primary Product:

The Point Line system integrates 2D, 3D and modeling into a system that has basic drafting functions and excellent design capabilities. The fast "fly-through" of a perspective drawing is a feature of the system. The system has been used more in the manufacturing area but is paying close attention to the architectural market.

Other Products:

Data management modules, paint program and utilities.

Robo Systems Corporation
111 Pheasant Run
Newtown, Pa 18940

215-968-4422

Primary Product:

Robocad PC is the latest product from this pioneer in the PC CAD business. Their earlier systems were designed to run on the Apple II while the new releases are for the IBM AT. The most unique attribute of the PC system is its bit mapped graphics screen with pull down menus which resemble the Apple Macintosh. The system is easy to use and powerful.

Other Products:

Apple based systems, modules and libraries.

T & W Systems Inc.
7372 Prince Drive, Suite 106
Huntington Beach, Ca 94133

800-228-2028

Primary Product:

VersaCAD is the oldest and most mature of the 2D CAD systems on the microcomputer and has extensive libraries of symbols, templates and options to offer the architectural user. The company has been a major supplier of microcomputer CAD systems starting with the premier Apple II system which is still a lively seller to schools. VersaCAD has an impressive programming language associated with it called CPL (for CAD programming language). This system works to its optimum when linked with a graphics tablet. The system will automatically generate overlays of symbol libraries which have been defined by the user.

Other Products:

VersaDATA fully integrated bidirectional alphanumeric database system. Extensive symbol libraries. Architectural overlay system. Macro libraries. Integrated 3D wireframe, surface and solids modeling. Apple II CAD systems.

"A" SIZE SHEET

8 1/2" x 11"

ABSOLUTE COORDINATES

Coordinates based on points measured from a fixed origin on X, Y or Z axes.

ACTIVE DRIVE

The diskette or drive that is accessed by the operating system (DOS). This might be A>, B> or C>. The active drive can be changed by typing C: or A: at the DOS prompt and then pressing RETURN.

ALIASING

The jaggies or the stairstep effect on a display with a resolution too low to reproduce diagonals and curves smoothly.

ANTIALIASING

Software designed to counteract the stairstep effect and make diagonal and curved lines display smoothly.

ASPECT RATIO

The ratio of CRT display width to display height.

ASCII

American National Standard Code for Information Interchange. This is the standard code used in computer files and to exchange data between various computer systems.

ATTRIBUTE

For most CAD systems this refers to a data item such as a value or character string assigned to a specific graphic item like a symbol. These attributes are assigned in ei:MicroSpec to Items.

AUTOMATIC DIMENSIONING

The ability of a CAD system to automatically measure distances and place extensions and dimension lines on the drawing.

AXIS

One of three perpendicular lines intersecting at a common point in space.

"B" SIZE SHEET

11" x 17".

BACKUP

Making an extra copy of a file or diskette in case the original is damaged or lost.

BILL OF MATERIALS

A list of parts represented in a drawing. In CAD this ability is usually automated.

BOOT

To start a computer in order to run a program or to start a program you wish to use while the computer is already running.

"C" SIZE SHEET

Architectural paper size is 24" x 36" and engineering is 22" x 34".

CAD

Computer Aided Drafting and Design software systems.

CAM

Computer Aided Manufacturing, where a computer is actually in control of manufacturing processes and machinery.

COORDINATES, CARTESIAN

Measurements in the world of CAD are done in relationship to the system of Cartesian coordinates named after French philosopher and mathematician Rene Descartes; the "axes" of the system are X representing length, Y representing width and Z representing height. The numbers which identify the location of a point in space are "coordinates."

COMMAND

In DOS and other computer programs, the keyboard or mouse entry that selects a menu item or instructs the computer to execute a specific operation.

CONFIGURE

To set up or install a software program or hardware and make the necessary settings to make the system operate properly.

COPROCESSOR

A coprocessor is a computer chip that aids the primary central processing unit in making the calculation necessary to process the information at hand. The central processing chips used in IBM PC's, such as the Intel 8088 and 80286, can not solve multiplication and division problems directly. These processes have to be done within the software. This slows dramatically the process of calculating vectors in a CAD drawing . The math coprocessor chips such as the 8087 and 80287 take over this process within the hardware and can speed the computations by many times.

CPU

Central Processing Unit, the main part of the computer that contains the main memory, control and processing.

CROSSHAIRS

The vertical and horizontal lines that focus on the point of attention in the drawing process. The cross hair is used both on the CRT screen and the puck of the digitizer.

CRT

The screen monitor used to display graphics and other information from the computer. It stands for Cathode Ray Tube.

CURSOR

The pointer on the computer screen that indicates where the next input is to occur. Usually in CAD it is a small cross or a full screen crosshair. In other programs it is a blinking dash.

"D" SIZE SHEET

30" x 42".

DATABASE

The body of computer data stored in the computer memory that constitutes information about the various projects, items, companies, catalogues and categories. The data in the computer are organized in rows (records) and columns (fields).

DATABASE EXTRACTION

The ability of a CAD system to read data values or attributes from a drawing file into a data file. These data can then be manipulated and sorted by dBASE III, or can be imported into ei:Microspec.

DEFAULT DRIVE

The diskette or drive that is automatically activated by the computer or program command unless a different drive is specified. Usually in DOS the default drive is A.

DEFAULT SETTINGS

In DOS, CAD, and other computer applications, values that a computer system will automatically assume unless different settings are specified in a COMMAND.

DIGITIZE

To convert coordinate information into digital form for processing by a computer. In CAD it is the process of indirectly or directly reading drawing information into the machine.

DIGITIZING TABLET

A magnetic tablet with a stylus pointer or puck with crosshairs used to digitize a drawing or input control information.

DIMENSIONING

Measurement and placement of dimensional information during the process of drawing.

DIRECTORY

A list of files on a diskette or hard disk, managed by DOS. A directory can have other directories in it, holding lists of other files. Directories are referred to by a "path" (e.g. \DIR 1\DIR 1A\).

DISK or DISKETTE

A storage medium on which data and program files are stored. "Disk" may be used to refer to either a floppy diskette or a "hard disk."

DOS

Acronym for Disk Operating System, the program that controls many personal computer functions. Before running most application software programs, you must first "boot" the Disk Operating System to get a computer system ready to run the program. DOS also executes the formatting and copy functions used to prepare diskettes to store information and to duplicate programs and data files.

DOS PROMPT

In DOS, usually a letter followed by a "greater than" sign (>); the appearance of a prompt indicates that the computer system is ready to execute another command, and typically the letter indicates which is the "active" drive.

DRIVE

A computer hardware device that stores and retrieves data on and from a floppy diskette or hard disk.

EDIT

The process of changing, adding or deleting information contained in a drawing or file.

ENTER

In DOS, CAD, and other computer applications, to type in required information from the keyboard, usually followed by pressing the carriage return key (RETURN).

ENTITIES

The basic drawing elements used to draw in CAD. The include lines, points, arcs, etc. and are also called "primitives."

ERASE

To remove information from the drawing or file.

EXIT

In DOS, CAD, and other computer applications, to end or leave a program and return to DOS, or to end or leave a procedure and return to the main program.

EXTENSION

In DOS, CAD, and other computer applications, the optional three-character addition to a filename (for example, the EXT in FILENAME.EXT). The same extension may be given to files in a generic group so that each remains distinct while all the files of a type may be managed as a group.

EXTRACTION

The process of counting and measuring graphic data, to isolate numeric values for use in determining the "real contents" of a drawing. Extraction typically passes symbol counts and layer line lengths as numeric values to estimate programs. Other "attributes" (such as color) may also be involved in the extraction process.

FIELD

A "column" in a conventional computer database -- a field designates the meaning of data held in a regular location in a computer database. Typically, fields are characterized by a width and type -- numeric, character, or logical (true/false). Numeric fields also typically have a number of places behind the decimal point.

FILE

In DOS, CAD, and other computer applications, a program or data group stored on a diskette or hard disk as a single unit and under one filename.

FILENAME

In DOS, CAD, and other computer applications, the name (of eight characters or less, optionally followed by a period and an extension of up to three characters -- for example, FILENAME.EXT) given to all files before they can be stored on a disk or diskette.

FILL

Coloring or shading or pattern of line segments applied to an entity or object in a drawing.

FLOATING POINT SYSTEM

A CAD program which keeps track of where objects are located using real numbers as opposed to integer numbers. This is the more common and more accurate system, however it is slower than the integer based systems. For architecture there is no accuracy problem for either system.

FORMAT

To prepare a diskette to store program or data files, using the DOS FORMAT command.

FRAME BUFFER

Memory device that stores display bit patterns between processing and display. This device enables a faster display of graphic information.

FUNCTION KEYS

Special keys located on the keyboard or ancillary to the keyboard with predefined operations associated with them.

GRAPHICS TABLET

The same as a digitizing tablet.

GROUP

Primitives which are operated on as a set with a single command.

HANDLE POINT

The graphic point where the cursor grabs on to an object or group to move or edit it.

HARD DISK

A nonremovable disk and its storage and retrieval mechanism, built into some computers, which is capable of storing many times the information that can be stored on a floppy diskette, and of processing it faster. A hard disk, also known as a fixed disk, is usually designated as Drive C.

HATCHING

Filling of an area in a drawing with a regular pattern of lines.

HIDDEN LINES

Lines in a 3D drawing that would be obscured from view or hidden by objects or planes between them and the viewer.

HIDDEN LINE REMOVAL

Complex programs that calculate which lines are "hidden" from the viewer at a specified viewer point and then systematically and automatically removed from the display or plot file.

ICON

A symbol representing a command or menu item.

IGES

Acronym for Initial Graphic Exchange Standard. This is the standard developed to allow digital graphic information to be shared between unlike programs and machines.

INDEX

An auxiliary file or other data structure that sorts and generally points to records in the order of a database field. An index can be given for each key field or combination of fields, where "key" refers to a unique record.

INPUT

Information entered into a computer system by means of the keyboard, mouse, digitizer, or other device.

INTERACTIVE

The ability of a computer user to operate on the data directly from the keyboard or other device. This is opposed to the earlier, more common batch processing method which required the user to prepare the data and return at a later time to view the results.

INTEGER BASED SYSTEM

CAD software that uses integers to refer to locations within its database. This system is not as accurate as floating point systems but can be much faster. For architectural purposes the accuracy is more than adequate.

JOYSTICK

A device for moving the cursor or selecting information on the CRT screen. This is similar in function to the mouse.

LAYER

A way of managing graphic data in groups. Layers may be edited, saved or plotted discretely or in any of various combinations. This data management method is similar to overlay drafting.

LIBRARY

A collection of graphic data or symbols which may be drawn upon to create elements of a drawing without redrawing.

LOAD

To move information stored on a diskette or hard disk into the memory of a computer.

MACRO

A group of commands that result in a predefined operation on the computer. These commands are invoked by a key, keyword or short keystroke combination and may be very complex.

MENU

In CAD and other computer applications, a list of options or commands displayed on screen from which the user chooses.

MIRROR

The flopping of an object to its mirror or opposite hand view.

MONITOR

The cathode ray tube used to display graphic and other information from the computer.

MOUSE

A hand held cursor control/input device attached to the computer.

NESTING

Associating an object with a group.

OBJECT

A drawing element such as a line or vector. Also called an entity or primitive.

OPERATING SYSTEM

The set of programs that manage routine device, disk and file maintenance procedures such as copying, deleting, formatting, and so forth. MS-DOS is the operating system for many PC's.

OUTPUT

The "product" of a computer program -- that is, the graphics or text information produced by using the program.

PAN

Moving the displayed area of a drawing horizontally or vertically.

PATH

The DOS specification of a directory and subdirectories (e.g. \DIR 1\DIR 1A). A single backslash, "\", indicates the root directory. Used to specify where files are located.

PERIPHERAL

Devices external but attached to the computer such as plotters, mice, printers, etc.

PIXEL

The smallest visible point on a raster display which can be controlled independently by the computer in regard to color or intensity level. The number of pixels per square inch is the degree of resolution of the CRT display.

PLOT

The hardcopy graphic output of the CAD system performed by a plotter or printer.

PLOTTER

The hardcopy graphic output device used to prepare a plot. The method used varies from computer controlled moving pens to eletrostatic processes similar to photocopy machines.

PRIMITIVES

The same as entities.

PROMPT

In DOS, CAD, and other computer applications, a request for information displayed by the program to let you know what is expected next. For example, the typical DOS prompt, "C>", indicates that DOS is waiting for your next command.

PUCK

The input device attached to a digitizer.

RASTER

A device which creates a graphic display or image from rows of dots or pixels.

RESOLUTION

The measure of accuracy of a display or plotting device. The measurement is expressed in pixels or dots per inch.

RUBBER BANDING

In CAD the apparent attachment of a line to the previously drawn object or line giving the user orientation. The line moves, expands and contracts as the cursor is moved until the next drawing element is placed, then it is fixed.

SECURITY DEVICE

In computer terminology, a device used to prevent unauthorized use and/or reproduction of software.

SNAP

An aspect of CAD programs that permits the cursor to go directly and precisely to the nearest grid point, vertex, user-defined increment between grid points or user defined node.

SYMBOL

In CAD, a graphic entity created out of other graphic objects. Symbols have one point of reference (called a basepoint) and are "placed" on one layer.

TOGGLE

Turning on or off a command by pressing the same key or command. It alters the state to the opposite condition.

VECTOR

A straight line with both direction (x, y, z) and magnitude and always defined by its two end points. Vectors are either absolute or relative.

WILD CARD

In DOS, a character (*) used in place of one or more specific characters in a filename to process several files with similar filenames. For example, the command DIR *.SYM will cause the computer to list all the files in the active drive.

WINDOW

A defined area on a CRT screen which may be smaller than the actual screen. Parts of a drawing or information can be displayed on the window while maintaining orientation. It is also used to refer to the process of zooming is on an area of a drawing or selecting an area for editing by graphic group.

ZOOM

To enlarge or reduce an area of the drawing in display.

LIST OF PLATES

Used with permission of:

Pages: 176, 177
AT&T

Pages: 81, 152, 153, 154, 155, 156
Autodesk, Inc.

Pages: 146, 147, 148, 149, 150, 151, 158, 159, 160, 169 170, 171, 172
Calcomp

Pages: 41, 43, 45, 47, 49, 51, 53, 57, 59, 61, 63, 65, 67, 69, 157
Creative Technologies Inc.

Pages: 15, 77, 79, 92, 96, 97, 117, 119, 161, 163, 175
Imagimedia Technologies, Inc.

Pages: 75, 91, 93, 94, 95, 178
MegaCAD, Inc.

Pages: 164, 165, 166, 167, 168
Microtecture Corporation

Pages: 173, 174
Robo Systems

Pages: 83, 85, 142, 143, 144, 145
T&W Systems

Unless noted above, all the illustrations in this book are by the author.

BOOKS OF RELATED INTEREST FROM WILLIAM KAUFMANN, INC.

Interior Architecture: Drafting and Perspective
Frederic H. Jones, Ph.D.
A must-have desktop reference. Covering almost every aspect of practical interior design graphics—from basic to advanced practices—this single volume serves as a refresher for the professional, a "how-to" for students, and a design resource for all. 240 pp.

Design Yourself
Kurt Hanks, Larry Belliston and David Edwards
This graphic book, loaded with games, exercises and fun projects, will help any reader analyze, plan, visualize and communicate. 140 pp.

Interior Design Graphics: Basics—Examples—Standards
Frederic H. Jones, Ph.D.
Demystifies the process of interior design drafting with basic instruction on how to draw interior design plans. 136 pp.

DRAW: A Visual Approach to Thinking, Learning and Communicating
Kurt Hanks and Larry Belliston
Contains 700 drawings, cartoons, sketches and photographs— exemplary visualizations from the simplest to the most complex—and brief, easy-to-grasp discussions of the essential tools, methods and techniques of modern drawing and design. 256 pp.

Rapid Viz: Techniques for Rapid Visualization
Kurt Hanks and Larry Belliston
Principles, methods and exercises for learning mastery of the "second language" of visual expression. 150 pp.

Wake Up Your Creative Genius
Kurt Hanks and Jay Parry
An invigorating short course in creativity designed to maximize the number of bright ideas that hit their targets. 180 pp.

Drawing Home Plans: A Simplified Drafting System for Planning and Design
June Curran
Shows beginners how to express their ideas on paper, in accurate scale, using universally understood symbols and instructs them in how to read blueprints and visualize plans drawn by others. 253 pp.

Notes on Architecutre
Michael Lee
The basics on structure, human scale materials, and the history of the field are covered in this concise introductory book. 48 pp.

Notes on Interior Design
Information Design Associates
A visual introduction to the field of interior design, stressing basic principles. 48 pp.

Designing Creative Resumes
Gregg Berryman
How to effectively prepare portfolios and resumes that will attract and sustain the interest of the prospective employer. 100 pp.

Notes on Graphic Design and Visual Communication
Gregg Berryman
Packed with essential design information, this notebook provides a basic "visual vocabulary" and helps launch further study of graphic design. Each topic is illustrated with select examples. 48 pp.

DATE DUE

APR 2 0 1990			
GAYLORD			PRINTED IN U.S.A.